A Guide to R for Social and Behavioral Science Statistics

Dedicated to the memory of Marissa McAneny Waclawski—she hated statistics

Sara Miller McCune founded SAGE Publishing in 1965 to support the dissemination of usable knowledge and educate a global community. SAGE publishes more than 1000 journals and over 800 new books each year, spanning a wide range of subject areas. Our growing selection of library products includes archives, data, case studies and video. SAGE remains majority owned by our founder and after her lifetime will become owned by a charitable trust that secures the company's continued independence.

Los Angeles | London | New Delhi | Singapore | Washington DC | Melbourne

A Guide to R for Social and Behavioral Science Statistics

Brian Joseph Gillespie

University of Groningen, Netherlands

Kathleen Charli Hibbert

U.S. Environmental Protection Agency

William E. Wagner, III

California State University, Channel Islands

Los Angeles | London | New Delhi
Singapore | Washington DC | Melbourne

FOR INFORMATION:

SAGE Publications, Inc.
2455 Teller Road
Thousand Oaks, California 91320
E-mail: order@sagepub.com

SAGE Publications Ltd.
1 Oliver's Yard
55 City Road
London, EC1Y 1SP
United Kingdom

SAGE Publications India Pvt. Ltd.
B 1/I 1 Mohan Cooperative Industrial Area
Mathura Road, New Delhi 110 044
India

SAGE Publications Asia-Pacific Pte. Ltd.
18 Cross Street #10-10/11/12
China Square Central
Singapore 048423

Acquisitions Editor: Leah Fargotstein
Editorial Assistant: Claire Laminen
Production Editor: Kelle Schillaci Clarke,
    Bennie Clark Allen
Copy Editor: Diane DiMura
Typesetter: Hurix Digital
Proofreader: Jennifer Grubba
Indexer: Sheila Hill
Cover Designer: Lysa Becker
Marketing Manager: Shari Countryman

Printed in the United States of America

Library of Congress Cataloging-in-Publication Data

Names: Gillespie, Brian Joseph, author. | Hibbert, Kathleen Charli, author. | Wagner, William E. (William Edward), author.

Title: A guide to R for social and behavioral science statistics / Brian Joseph Gillespie, University of Groningen, Netherlands, Kathleen Charli Hibbert, William E. Wagner, III, California State University, Channel Islands.

Description: Thousand Oaks, California : SAGE, [2021] | Includes bibliographical references.

Identifiers: LCCN 2019047132 | ISBN 9781544344027 (paperback ; alk. paper) | ISBN 9781544344003 (epub) | ISBN 9781544344010 (epub) | ISBN 9781544344034 (epub)

Subjects: LCSH: Social sciences--Statistical methods. | Psychology—Statistical methods. | R (Computer program language)

Classification: LCC HA29 .G529 2021 | DDC 519.50285/5133—dc23 LC record available at https://lccn.loc.gov/2019047132

This work is not a product of the U.S. Government or the U.S. Environmental Protection Agency, and the author/editor/speaker is not doing this work in any governmental capacity. The views expressed are those of the author/editor/speaker only and do not necessarily represent those of the U.S. Government or the EPA.

This book is printed on acid-free paper.

20 21 22 23 24 10 9 8 7 6 5 4 3 2 1

BRIEF CONTENTS

DETAILED CONTENTS

PREFACE

PURPOSE OF THE BOOK

The book was designed to be an accessible social/behavioral science statistics text that contains information on intermediate-level statistics used by undergraduates and graduate students using the R statistical language and software. The text is an ideal introduction to R for data science students familiar with introductory statistical concepts and professionals looking to learn R without computer science experience. The text is largely descriptive, with worked examples using RStudio and data from the 2016 wave of the *General Social Survey* (GSS). Supplemental files on the book's website (https://study.sagepub.com/researchmethods/statistics/gillespie-r-for-statistics) include a subset of the GSS data and R code for each chapter of the book. With this book, you will be able to practice writing R code to open data, produce visualizations and data summaries, conduct basic statistical analyses, and write up the results of your analyses.

Each chapter in the book provides a reasonable amount of conceptual overview. In particular, Chapter 6 reviews hypothesis testing and effect size because this information is crucial as a foundation for what is covered in later chapters. Students and instructors using this book exclusively as an R supplement should feel comfortable skipping this section, as it does not contain any references to R or RStudio. However, the concepts are indeed essential for accurately interpreting the results of the statistical analyses in Chapters 7 through 12.

OTHER FEATURES

- Screenshots for common menu-based commands within the RStudio GUI.
- Sidebars that annotate specific parts of sample code and output.

NOTES ON R

As with other statistical analysis software, there are often several ways to conduct the same statistical analyses. In these chapters, we have chosen to highlight only one or—at most—two methods to conduct a given analysis. The decisions for which method we chose are that which seem most intuitive to an introductory R user.

We do not draw too heavily on the incredible and impressive library of user-created R packages unless it is necessary to complete a given command. Instead, the examples in this book use RStudio and what are known as "Base R" commands, or "out-of-the-box" R functions. However, there are instances where complex calculations can be completed with the use of R packages, the "after-market" R functions that facilitate more advanced operations. In those cases, we explain how to install and "read" the packages into R as well as interpret their documentation. This topic is introduced and explored further in Chapter 1.

While R code has cross-platform compatibility (i.e., Windows and Mac), some of the techniques—particularly keystroke commands—will be relevant only to Windows users.

TIPS FOR LEARNING R

R uses command-line scripting (code) to do data management, conduct statistical analyses, and produce graphics. This is both useful and important for at least two reasons. First, writing and running code allows for more control over the process of what is being done, especially when compared with point-and-click menu-based statistical applications. Second, writing code allows for a more complete and detailed record of what has been done from beginning to end. Therefore, code can be checked for errors, rerun, shared with others, reused with similar data, and statistical analyses can be easily reproduced. Keep in mind these three "general rules," which will help you become more comfortable with writing and running R code:

Keep code broken down into small modules. The program will do everything you want it to do but only when the code is error free. Keeping the code for your analyses in small chunks helps to see what is being run and how it is done. Also, this "small-chunks" approach makes problem code much easier to spot and fix when something is not working.

Comment on your code to show your paper trail. As you will see throughout this book, we have relied heavily on commenting for the code we provide to you. Keeping detailed comments about your coding decisions is important for a number of reasons. First, it will help you remember decisions you made (and why you made them). Second, you can share the code with collaborators who can then edit and share with you. Third, you and others can more easily replicate your work. As mentioned above, there are many ways to do the same thing in R—so keeping a detailed record of your decisions makes clear which path you chose and why.

At first, do not simply copy/paste code. Although we provide all of our R code on the book's website, try typing it out by hand into the RStudio GUI. This will help you get used to the practice of writing code.

Code, Output, and Annotation Conventions

Within the book, we have a number of conventions about how we present information. When we name a variable within the GSS 2016, we will use the Courier New font (e.g., sei10). Code used to conduct statistical analysis is also presented `in blue Courier New font`. Notes for the code is printed in black Lucida Grande font. Additional text notes, including helpful tips, are presented in the margins of the text. Packages and commands are presented in **bold**.

> Lastly, output is printed in black font in a table box separate from the text.

OVERVIEW

This book works in four parts. Part I introduces you to R and the basic functions of the RStudio statistical application, which we use to conduct statistical analyses throughout the rest of the book. The book then moves on to a chapter on data management. Here, we discuss how to clean and "handle" data prior to conducting statistical analyses. Part II begins with an introduction to the most basic approach to statistical analysis, *descriptive statistics*. Accordingly, the chapters within this section introduce you to frequencies, measures of central tendency and variability, and ways to create effective visual representations of your data. Part III discusses common *inferential statistics*, which are used when researchers want to draw inferences about a population of people from a sample. Part IV continues the discussion of inferential statistics but shifts to a specific type of analysis—correlation and regression. In each chapter, we (a) discuss a common statistical procedure and when it is appropriate to use it and (b) provide detailed instructions and code for how to conduct the analysis in R using RStudio.

ACKNOWLEDGMENTS

The authors would like to thank Leah Fargotstein, Claire Laminen, Kelle Clarke, and the production and design teams at SAGE Publications for their help making this book. We also acknowledge the support of our family and friends, especially Janet Lever, Clara Mulder, Patrick and Joe Griffin, John Whiteley, Cambria and Daniel Hibbert, Shannon Koplitz, Erin Ruel, Vicente Torres, and Justin Huang.

We would like to acknowledge the work of accuracy checker D. Adeline Yeh, who diligently checked the R code and output against the copy for this book. We appreciate each of the reviewers for their thoughtful comments on earlier drafts of the manuscript.

Kurt J. Beron, The University of Texas at Dallas

Richard Blisset, Seton Hall University

Zhuo Job Chen, Clemson University

Renato Corbetta, University of Alabama at Birmingham

Scott Crawford, University of Wyoming

Fernando DePaolis, Middlebury Institute of International Studies

Michael W. Frank, Anderson University

David Han, The University of Texas at San Antonio

Lisa Hollis-Sawyer, Northeastern Illinois University

Ahmed Ibrahim, Johns Hopkins University

Ho Hon Leung, SUNY Oneonta

Catherine Pearsall, St. Joseph's College

Charles Plante, University of Saskatchewan

Steven V. Rouse, Pepperdine University

Shayna Rusticus, Kwantlen Polytechnic University

Frank A. Salamone, Iona College and University of Phoenix

Oreta M. Samples, Fort Valley State University

Erika Wells, Boston University

Kyle M. Woosnam, University of Georgia

Zhiwei Zhu, University of Louisiana at Lafayette

ABOUT THE AUTHORS

Brian Joseph Gillespie, Ph.D. is a researcher in the Faculty of Spatial Sciences at the University of Groningen in the Netherlands. He is the author of *Household Mobility in America: Patterns, Processes, and Outcomes* (Palgrave, 2017) and coauthor of *The Practice of Survey Research: Theory and Applications* (SAGE, 2016) and *Using and Interpreting Statistics in the Social, Behavioral, and Health Sciences* (SAGE, 2018). He has published research in a variety of social science journals on topics related to family, migration, the life course, and interpersonal relationships.

Kathleen Charli Hibbert, Ph.D. is a social ecologist at the U.S. Environmental Protection Agency researching potential health impacts from relationships and interactions between humans and their environment(s). She has published works on micro-activity behavior, intentional living communities, vulnerable communities, e-waste, non-chemical stressors, children's health, and older adult sexuality. She has taught quantitative analysis and research methods in sociology, psychology, and research departments using a variety of statistical applications.

William E. Wagner, III, M.A., M.P.H., Ph.D. holds a joint appointment as Professor of Health Sciences and Professor of Sociology at California State University–Channel Islands where he teaches courses in statistics and research methods. He has published research on topics such as health behavior, urban sociology, sports, homophobia, and academic status. He is co-author of *Using and Interpreting Statistics in the Social, Behavioral, and Health Sciences* (SAGE, 2018), *Adventures in Social Research*, 10e (SAGE, 2018), and *The Practice of Survey Research* (SAGE, 2016), and author of *Using IBM® SPSS® Statistics for Research Methods and Social Science Statistics* (2019).

R AND RSTUDIO®

INTRODUCTION

This chapter begins our exploration of social science data and statistics using R. While this book may be used as a companion with another statistics resource, it can also stand alone as a basic introductory statistics guide integrated with instructions for how to utilize the components of R to calculate statistics, produce graphical and tabular output, and to interpret these elements that are produced.

Here, we introduce readers to the object-oriented framework in R and RStudio and provide instructions on how to download and install the applications. We utilize screenshots to identify and explore the four primary windows within R/RStudio and discuss details about their basic functions. Although this book does not make use of user-created packages available in R/RStudio, we demonstrate how to search for, download, and install or uninstall packages as needed. We also introduce the **tidyverse** package and provide examples of how to read R user-created package documentation. We then provide step-by-step instructions for opening data in .txt, .csv, and URL formats and saving the data files for later use.

STATISTICAL SOFTWARE OVERVIEW

There are many options available for individuals seeking computer software to perform statistical analysis as well as data management. Some of the more popular software packages include IBM's SPSS Statistics, the SAS System, and Stata. R is a type of computer programming language. This computer programming language can be used to organize and analyze data and employ statistical techniques. Using R, one can also utilize basic calculations in the same way that most computer programming language can perform calculations such as addition, subtraction, multiplication, and division.

By almost all accounts, R is much more difficult to use than the major statistical packages available for purchase. Its interface is neither pleasant nor nimble. Its output is not as elegant. Moreover, there is a much steeper learning curve with R than with, say, SPSS Statistics. To make matters worse, for a student learning statistics while having also to deal with the particulars and peculiarities of R, this might seem like a daunting task, especially by comparison to learning statistics with a popular commercial software package (e.g., SPSS Statistics). Also, SPSS Statistics is far more widely used in most classroom environments. However, once the learning curve is overcome, R is a very powerful statistical tool. Moreover, R is gaining in popularity.

Having said all that, it has one tremendous advantage over SPSS Statistics, the SAS System, Stata, and many other packages. Its price simply cannot be beat—R is free. That alone is enough to merit an investigation into its capabilities and explore opportunities that this type of programming language may offer for perhaps more flexibility than other software packages in particular applications. That is to say that R can be used for basic, traditional statistical analysis, but it can also be used for more advanced and less mainstream statistical analysis.

As you begin and continue further along on your journey of understanding statistics and the R software, you will begin to understand how to make things happen, things that may not seem clear or intuitive at all when you first begin. Similarly, you will also gain awareness of the kinds of things that can be done with R and how to facilitate those with a design that you can lay out in a "logical" way. To gain this understanding of the logic of the programming will take some time and understanding, particularly of the basic functions and operations with the R programming language. To be fair, while SPSS Statistics and the others are more intuitive and have more bells and whistles, there are times when using a programming language makes things work more smoothly. One example of this would be if you need recode multiple variables in a similar fashion. With the complex GUI (graphical user interface) in SPSS Statistics, for instance, you would need to go through the process by point-and-click steps each time, for each separate variable. With programming languages, it's typically a far more elegant process involving copying and pasting with some editing of the pasted code.

Granted, this can be done using the "Syntax" option with SPSS. (This option is not available for the limited use student version.) Many users either do not know how to do that or find it difficult to switch back and forth. With R, you will become accustomed to the programming approach and, despite the steep learning curve, you will no doubt be rewarded with knowledge of faster and easier ways to do some of the more basic statistical and data management tasks.

In addition, many skilled users of R feel that typing the code to produce their output is almost always faster than dealing with the GUI. (Note that there is a GUI with RStudio, to be addressed in the next section, but it is not intended to be at the same level of those of the popular commercial statistical software packages. Its purpose will be revealed shortly.) For the complex GUIs to accomplish what is produced with programming code, a series of windows, check boxes, and other visual tools are used. The process of going through these, while much more intuitive, actually takes more time. The point here is to indicate that not only is R free, but after you become more familiar with the application, R might actually suit your needs better than other programs, particularly if you are or become a regular user of statistical software.

To that end, let us first download and install the software.

DOWNLOADING R AND RSTUDIO

R

To download R software, visit this website: https://www.r-project.org/

Choose the download CRAN selection on the menu to the left. CRAN means Comprehensive R Archive Network. There will be a list of "mirror" sites, representing servers around the world where you can download the free software. Choose the one closest to your location to get started. Then, select the appropriate version for your computer (e.g., Linux, MacOS X, Windows). Once you have downloaded the package, follow the instructions and install the software on your computer.

Once you click the download link, you will be presented with a list of server locations from where you can download the software.

Since we are downloading the application in Los Angeles, California, we chose the link at UCLA (University of California, Los Angeles). After selecting the closest mirror link, you will be presented with the following window, where you can select the type of computer on which you will be using R:

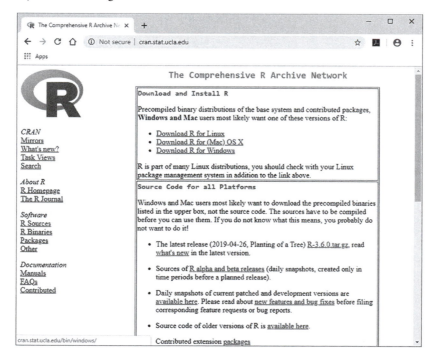

The last step in the download process for R is to choose the correct installation package. First, note that we will download the base package.

> **Tip:** While you will notice that, in our example, the latest download version is 3.6.0, the version number will change as updated versions are released.

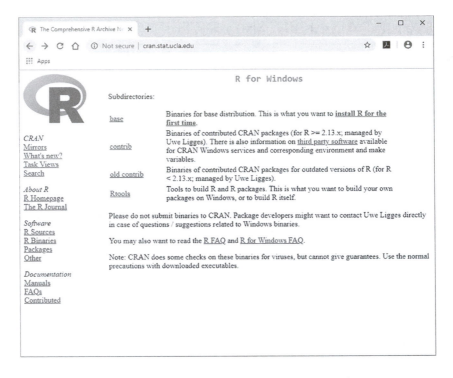

Now that you have downloaded the software, you will need to install it on your computer.

Follow these steps:

1. Click the icon for "R-3.6.0.pkg".

2. The following window will appear—read the license agreement and select "Next >".

3. Choose the directory where you would like to install R; then click "Next >".

4. Select components to install. You may choose to install only 32- or 64-bit files, depending on the machine you are using. For this example, we will download both. Select "Next >".

5. You will have the option to customize startup options. As a beginning user, we recommend to click "No," which accepts the default options. Then, click "Next >".

Setup - R for Windows 3.6.0   —   □   ✕

Startup options
Do you want to customize the startup options?

Please specify yes or no, then click Next.

○ Yes (customized startup)
◉ No (accept defaults)

< Back   Next >   Cancel

6. Determine in which folder of the startup menu you would like to have R shortcuts located and then click "Next >".

Setup - R for Windows 3.6.0   —   □   ✕

Select Start Menu Folder
Where should Setup place the program's shortcuts?

Setup will create the program's shortcuts in the following Start Menu folder.

To continue, click Next. If you would like to select a different folder, click Browse.

R   Browse...

☐ Don't create a Start Menu folder

< Back   Next >   Cancel

7. Make your final selections and then click "Next >" to install R.

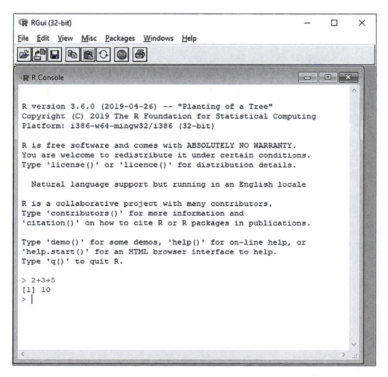

8. You are now ready to launch R.

Once you launch R, you will be presented with the R console. There is a prompt where you are able to enter commands or instructions to tell R what you would like it to calculate or create. In the console image below, you will see an example using simple arithmetic: "2+3+5" was entered and then R returned "10".

In its most basic form, R can function like a calculator, but our purpose of downloading R goes far beyond just simple calculations. This, however, is a good opportunity to become comfortable entering commands/instructions into R's console. For example, if you want to calculate the average of a group of numbers, you can enter them, within parentheses, and then divide by how many numbers there are. For example,

```
(5+4+9+10+6+21+1)/7
```

```
8
```

R added the numbers together and then divided by 7, yielding the mean for the distribution—8.

RSTUDIO

Before installing RStudio, you must install R ("base R"). We have already done this in the previous section, so now we proceed with the installation of RStudio.

To download RStudio, visit the following website: http://www.rstudio.com and click the button marked "Download R Studio". Here, you are presented with some choices— some free, others for a charge. We will download the free version for Desktop; you will have the choice of Windows, Mac OS, Ubuntu 32- or 64-bit, Fedora 32- or 64-bit. Depending on your machine, choose an operating system, download the file, and click the installer.

> **Tip:** In the Mac OS environment, you will need to click on the RStudio icon and drag it into the "Applications" folder right next to it. This will move the program to the Applications folder on your computer. In a Windows environment, there is a simple wizard to guide your installation; follow the three screens of the installation wizard.

Now you have another free software package on your computer: RStudio.

Note that the Console window, on the left, functions exactly as the console in the base R software that we began to explore earlier in this chapter. You can use basic arithmetic functions in exactly the same way. RStudio offers an environment that is a little bit friendlier than just a basic console.

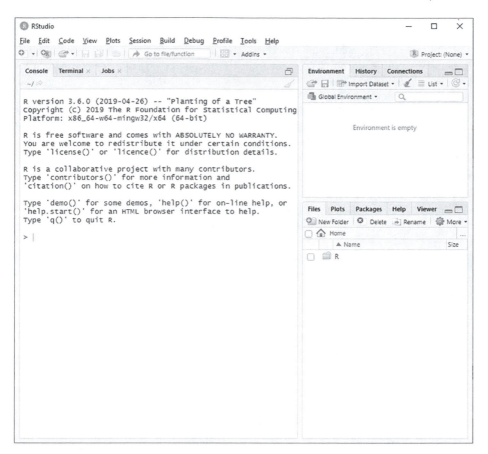

Introduction to RStudio

RStudio is an integrated development environment for R; as such, it is a requirement that you first have installed the base R software. After following the instructions in the previous section to install RStudio, you will notice at first glance, RStudio looks a bit more like typical modern computer programs/applications than does the base R package. There are more menus to choose from at the top of the screen; this means that there are some more options for completing tasks that can be carried out by pointing and clicking, or at least initially starting off with a point-and-click approach. Also, as you can see in the image below, the RStudio window is actually comprised of three separate windows. More discussion of the GUI (graphical user interface) from within the RStudio environment will be discussed in the next section, RStudio GUI.

RStudio GUI

The acronym, GUI (graphical user interface), may make it seem like R has now been transformed into a different sort of program and will function exactly like, for instance, SPSS Statistics. This is not the case. However, the RStudio GUI does make many things a bit easier to understand and, among other advantages, the GUI often makes it simpler to manage data and other files.

You will notice that there are several windows within the RStudio main window console. RStudio has the capability to change the location or order of these smaller windows, or panes. To do that, you can follow these menus on a Windows computer:

PC: Tools → Global Options

Macintosh: RStudio → Preferences

In the Options window above, you are able to change not only the organization of the panes within the larger window, but you also have the option to pick and choose menu options within some of those panes. We are not going to make any adjustments here for now, but this is something you might find helpful in the future, depending on which features of RStudio you most frequently use.

The Help Function

There is more than one way to get to the help you need. Here, we will discuss three ways to seek help from within R and RStudio.

First, you can use the programming code in the terminal window to summon help. That command is

```
help.start()
```

After clicking return, you will notice that a help window has been opened in the lower right [default] window pane. Here, you can begin to explore the options within the Help function. These will be described in more detail below.

If you are interested in guidance for working with a particular command, simply type a question mark and then the command. For example, if you want guidance concerning the **getwd()** command, you would type the following:

```
? getwd
```

Second, if you cannot recall or do not know the name of a specific command, but instead want to find relevant commands for a particular task or function, you obviously cannot use "?" method. Instead, you can use the Help search engine, described in detail below. This can be accessed using the **help.start()** command.

Help → R Help

After selecting the help option, you will see that the [default] lower right pane now shows a variety of links, which provide different types of help support.

Third, notice that within the pane on the lower right side of the main window, there are some menu tabs at the top. The default menus are "Files," "Plots," "Packages," "Help," and "Viewer." If you select the Help tab, you will see how to access the R Help portal in RStudio. If you've accessed the Help function at an earlier time or if you are using a shared computer and/or software package, then it is possible that someone else has used the Help function at some earlier point in time and what appears may be different from what is shown in the window pane below.

To get back to the Help homepage, you can click on the "Home" icon; this icon looks like a house and can be found in the row underneath the menus for this pane (Files, Plots, Packages, Help, Viewer). There are also forward and reverse arrows that function like a Web browser window, allowing you to go back and review pages already seen and then go forward again.

The Help portal offers a number of different kinds of assist, depending upon your predicament. For example, there are resources specific to R and RStudio. Resources to help you learn to use R to complete specific tasks are also available, including user manuals provided under the heading "Manuals."

What might be comforting and familiar within this group of helpful resources is that there is a search engine that operates in a way you might be familiar with while using other software packages: It provides a way to search for specifically what you are looking for. To reach this search engine, you may need to scroll down in that lower right pane a bit. You will see a heading called "Reference." Under the Reference heading, you will see an option for "Search Engine & Keywords."

Click on the "Search Engine & Keywords" link and you will find yourself at the R Search Engine prompt, as illustrated here:

Using the available box, you have the option to type in a word, words, or phrases just as you would with any search engine. Beneath the search box, you will see that there are choices to make the search more specific. In the first line, "Fields," you are able to mark the boxes of the areas where the engine will search for your term. You can choose to ask the search engine to return results that appear in topics, titles, concepts, or keywords. Depending on the frequency of the term(s) you are using to search, this may allow you to limit an unwieldy amount of search results or to increase an insufficient search result for terms that might be less common.

Among the options, you can ignore the letter case for your search terms, which means the search will be restricted based on whether or not the words are capitalized. The options under "Types" indicate where you will be linked in the search results, including standard help pages, vignettes, or demonstrations.

If you scroll further down through this window, you will see other sections, such as "Concepts" and "Keywords." Keywords provides a list of keywords that have been entered into the system, which return useful information in Help searches. You can click directly on any of the keywords and you will be taken to a list of associated pages. Depending on the nature of your need for help, this might be an effective strategy to begin browsing for assistance.

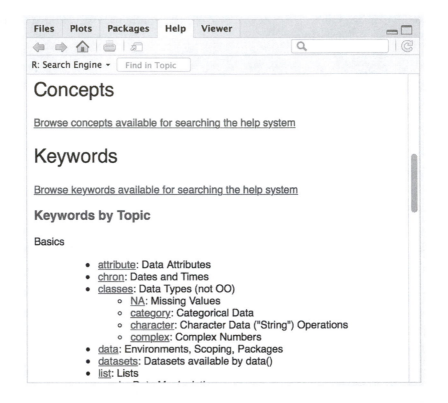

R is essentially a group of base commands packaged as "base R," with a multitude of packages available to be added on to the baseline version. Part of what makes this interesting is that each user may customize the packages that are included and so each instance of R across multiple computers might be very different. This can also make getting help a bit more complicated in some cases. One way to streamline that might be to begin with the "Packages" menu in the lower right window pane. Here, you will be shown a list of packages. By clicking on any of those links, you will be taken to a page that will provide a documentation file and then a list of Help pages related to that particular package.

FINDING R AND RSTUDIO PACKAGES

As discussed above, R is a software package that consists of base R. We have added the RStudio package which ensconces the base R within an interface that is a bit more pleasing, in that it offers a bit more point and click functionality, rather than relying solely on programming commands within the base R program. There are many other packages that can be added to customize the abilities of your version of R. In fact, your version of R can be as unique as you like it to be, in terms of the setting, format, and screen layout. It can also be as unique as you like in terms of the packages you choose to add to your base R.

Base R Packages

You can find R packages to run specific commands (based on your needs) at the following website: https://cran.r-project.org/web/packages/

At the time of this writing, there are over 13,000 packages identified at this site. For a complete list, you can select either the link, "Table of available packages, sorted by date of publication" or "Table of available packages, sorted by name." By clicking on the package name, you will be directed to a webpage where you will find a short description of the package in addition to links to download the package, along with other documentation.

RStudio Packages

R packages can also be found through the RStudio website, or directly at the following link: https://www.rstudio.com/products/rpackages/

Here, you will find a variety of project site links. When you click on any of these links, you are directed to a separate website established for that particular package. That page contains detailed information about the package, how to install, and how to seek help. Since these packages are all distinct projects, there is not a unifying single template for these websites.

Information will be presented in different formats across the packages with varying degrees of detail. In general, there are sufficient details to get started—often these details include information about how to utilize the package in more complex ways.

The Tidyverse

One suite of packages that appears on the RStudio site is called *tidyverse*. **Tidyverse** is a collection of packages that comprise the tidyverse core. As of the release of tidyverse 1.2.0, these include the following: **ggplot2**, **dplyr**, **tidyr**, **readr**, **purrr**, **tibble**, **stringr**, and **forcats**. Information on each of the packages that are included in the tidyverse can be found at the following link: https://www.tidyverse.org/packages/

> **Tip:** There are a few other packages included in the **tidyverse**, but less frequently used. For instance, if you are familiar with or have used other popular statistical packages, you will appreciate a particular package among this group called *haven*. This package assists users importing data files from the most popular commercial statistical packages: SPSS Statistics, SAS, and Stata.

To install the collection of packages in the **tidyverse**, you can enter the following on the command line in the R console window:

```
install.packages("tidyverse")
```

After you enter the command, you will be given information in the console about what files have been downloaded and where they are located on your machine. The next step is to attach the packages to your version of R. To do this, enter the following on the command line in the console window pane:

```
library (tidyverse)
```

Tip: Note that the package is case sensitive.

Now, you will get output in the console window such as that shown in the following image:

Notice that the eight core **tidyverse** packages have been attached to the R package on your machine. Online documentation generally offers information about downloading, installing, and using the package.

OPENING DATA

R is like any other major statistical package—in order to make calculations or produce graphical or tabular output, data are required. In this section, we will focus on opening existing data files.

It is important to consider the format of data files. R can store and retrieve data files that are comma separated values files, with the suffix .csv. With the help of additional packages, R can also handle other file formats from commercial statistical packages. From whatever format the data are drawn, it is important to consider where the data are located, as well. You will need to set the working directory to match the location of the data. Alternatively, you can download data directly from the Web.

Opening Existing Data

Using R command codes, it is first necessary to locate the data file that we plan to open. To determine the current working directory (i.e., the file folder where R will look for data or save data), you can enter the following on the command line in the R console window pane:

```
getwd()
```

In this case, R returned the following location:

```
"C:/Users/Desktop"
```

Since this is not where the data file that we need to access is located, it is necessary to change the working directory. This can be done by entering the following on the command line in the console window pane:

```
setwd("C:/Users/Desktop/R")
```

If the function was a success, nothing will happen. Another command line prompt ">" will appear beneath the line where you have typed the **setwd** command.

If, however, there was an error that prevented the change from being made, R will inform you of the error:

```
Error in setwd("C:/Users/Desktop/Rbook/"): cannot change
working directory
```

If you did not receive an error message, but would like to verify that the working directory has indeed been changed, you can do that very easily by, again, typing getwd() on the command line. It should return the directory that you have just set.

Now that the current working directory has been set, you are ready to read in the data file. Using the command line, one way to do this is by setting the active data file equal to the dataset that you have identified. In this case, we have identified the dataset this will be made available to you with this book and will be used with examples throughout the chapters. This is the *General Social Survey* (GSS) (Smith, Davern, Freese, & Morgan, 2019) 2016 file. This can be done entering the following command:

```
GSS2016 <- read.csv("GSS2016.csv")
```

> **Tip:** In later chapters, we list the entire filepath to the data—however, setting the working directory is a useful way to bypass listing all of the embedded folders leading to the location of the data.

If there is a problem, R will provide an error code to let you know that there was a problem. If no error code has been provided, then your operation was likely a success. We can see if the active data file has been set to the GSS2016 file in the upper right window pane. As seen below, it will show GSS2016 and indicate the number of observations (cases) and variables that are contained in the file.

If you look at the Menu tabs in the window from above, you will notice that there is a pull down menu labeled, "Import Dataset." This point-and-click method can also be employed to open an existing file. You will see that there are two options available to open text files: "From Text (base) . . ." and "From Text (readr) . . . ." Either one of these options will work.

The base option is a little less sophisticated than the readr option, which has a slightly more user-friendly window interface for the import process. First, we will try the base option. Click the Import Dataset drop-down menu and then select From Text (base), as shown in the following screenshot.

After making that selection, you will be given the option to locate a file on your machine. This might be on a hard disk, a flash drive, a network drive, or however you typically access your data files. After locating the data file and selecting it, you will be taken to the next window:

Here, you need to determine whether to use the first line of data for variable names or whether there are not variable names in this file and the data begins on line one. If there are variables names in the first line, then the "Yes" radio button next to "Heading" should be selected. If, however, there are not variable names in the file, then be sure to choose the "No" radio button next to "Heading."

> **Tip:** The data frame shown here reveals that the bolded first row contains variable names (headings) as "Yes" had been selected for "Heading" in this window. If "No" had been selected, those variable names would not be bolded and variable name placeholders (e.g., var1, var2, . . .) would have been used instead.

Now, try the same operation, but use the alternative option—readr. Click the drop-down menu for "Import Dataset", then from the list, choose "From Text (readr) . . . ." At this point, you will be shown a window to locate your data file. Since we are looking for a data file on our machine, you can click the "Browse . . ." button and you will then be able to navigate to the location of your file. Here, you will need to make a determination about whether variable names are included in the first row of the data file. If the first row of your data file contains variable names, be sure to check the box labeled, "First Row as Names." If the first row of your data file does not contain variable names, make sure that box is unchecked.

If your data file does contain variable names as the first line of delimited data, but you do not want to use those variables names, you can import the data and omit the variable names by making sure that the "First Row as Names" is not checked AND the fill-in-box next to "Skip:" is changed from a 0 to a 1. This will drop the top row down from variable name to data case, but the first row will then be skipped.

> **Tip:** Another helpful feature of this window is that the "Code Preview:" pane at the bottom of the window exhibits the command code that will be executed once this dialog box is completed. In other words, this is the command code that would be entered into the Console to complete the task without any point-and-click guidance.

Importing Other Formats

Data other than *.csv files can also be imported into R. This can be done with the help of the (**haven**) package. In this example, we show code to read in an SPSS Statistics data file to R. The following command code would be entered in the R console:

```
library(haven)
   newdata <- read_sav("~/Desktop/SPSS/data files/newdata.sav")
   View(newdata)
```

> **Tip:** This is just to provide sample code for this process since we do not provide additional SPSS data for these examples.

The image above shows what is delivered to the upper left pane of the R Studio window. Of course, this can also be achieved using the "Import Dataset" drop-down menu. When selecting "Import Dataset", scroll down and choose "From SPSS . . ." You will be presented with a window like the one you received when opening a CSV file. Follow along the same instructions to open your file in R.

Reading Data From a URL

A data file located at a URL is opened in a similar way to a data file on your computer. The only real difference is specifying that there is a URL. The following command code can be used to open data. In the event that you wanted to open an SPSS Statistics data file on the Web at https://study.sagepub.com/system/files/demo.sav, the following command code works just the same as if it were located on your computer or an attached drive:

```
library(haven)
  demo <-
  read _ sav("https://study.sagepub.com/system/files/demo.sav")
  View(demo)
```

Entering Data

The process of entering a large amount of data into R can be extremely cumbersome. Frankly, it is often more efficient to create a data file with another program and read it in to R. However, it is certainly possible to enter data into R directly. One way is through use of the command line. Suppose we need to create a data file with two variables, *x* and *y*. Further suppose that each of those variables has five cases, corresponding to scores on two exams taken by five individuals. Including the scores themselves, below you will find the command code to produce the variables, populated with the data, within R:

```
x <- c(65,85,90,100,85)
y <- c(77,72,88,65,82)
```

Once that is done, you can see the values have been added to the upper right pane of the R window:

		Project: (None) ▾
Environment	History	▬ ☐
📂 🖫 ⬛Import Dataset ▾	🧹	☰ List ▾ ⟳
🔵 Global Environment ▾	🔍	
Data		
▶ GSS2016	2867 obs. of 208 variables	▦
Values		
x	num [1:5] 65 85 90 100 85	
y	num [1:5] 77 72 88 65 82	

Once the data have been entered, you can perform operations, calculate statistics, and so on. For example, if you wanted to calculate the correlation between *x* and *y* (the procedure is discussed in a later chapter), you would enter cor (*x*, *y*), and the following result would be returned:

```
cor (x, y)
```

```
-0.276335
```

SAVING DATA FILES

One way to save data is by quitting R. This is done either by typing "quit()" in the console at the command prompt or by closing the R window or using the computer menus (command + Q in Mas OS; alt + F4 in MS Windows). When prompted to "Save workspace image?," be sure to click "Yes" and all of your data will be saved for next time.

One way to save a data file for use on another computer—or to share with others perhaps working on a different machine—is to use the **save()** command. This command code can be used to save one or more R objects to .rda file format. This data file can be read back into an instance of R using the **load()** command.

Suppose you have created new variables as independent objects in the workspace. In order to save them along with the data file, they first need to be aggregated. This can be done with the following command code, which aggregates the variables into a data frame, testscoresdata:

```
Testscoresdata <- data.frame(x, y)
view(testscoresdata)
```

Now to save the newly created data file, you can use the following command code:

```
save(testscoresdata, file = "testscores.RData")
```

The new file will be saved to the workspace directly as an R data file. R data files can always be loaded using the **load()** command.

You can take this opportunity to save the *General Social Survey* 2016 data (Smith et al., 2019) that was loaded in as a .csv file; it can now be saved as a *.Rdata file. Use the following command to save the file as a native R data file:

```
save(GSS2016, file = "GSS.RData")
```

> **Tip:** We will be importing the .csv file each time we load the data since these are the data that are available on this book's website: https://study.sagepub.com/researchmethods/statistics/gillespie-r-for-statistics

CONCLUSION

R is a programming language designed to analyze data. While R can be a bit unwieldy, RStudio is software that makes R a bit more intuitive—and perhaps a bit more accessible for most users. Going further, there are "packages" such as *tidyverse* that can be added to RStudio to help standardize tasks so that the wheel need not be reinvented for each job. Still, R will not be as polished or intuitive as commercial statistics software, such as SPSS Statistics; however, R does have the advantage of being free and it can be a powerful and flexible way to analyze data for patient users. In this chapter, we have given you the tools to embark on your journey with R. Throughout the rest of this book, we explain how to use R to accomplish a wide range of data analysis activities.

References

Smith, T. W., Davern, M., Freese, J., & Morgan, S. L. (2019). *General Social Surveys, 1972–2018* [Machine-Readable Data File]. Chicago, IL: NORC at the University of Chicago. Retrieved from http://www.gss.norc.org/getthedata/Pages/Home.aspx

Supplementary Digital Content

Download datasets and R code at the companion website at https://study.sagepub.com/researchmethods/statistics/gillespie-r-for-statistics

DATA, VARIABLES, AND DATA MANAGEMENT

ABOUT THE DATA AND VARIABLES

The data used throughout this book come from a selection of variables in the 2016 *General Social Survey* (GSS) (Smith, Davern, Freese, & Morgan, 2019). The full GSS dataset consists of 2867 responses to 208 variables and are made available for public use. If you have questions regarding the variables or the coding, we recommend that you download the *General Social Survey* codebook as a supplemental resource to use as you work through this book's examples. The full codebook can be downloaded from the following website: http://gss.norc.org/documents/codebook/GSS_Codebook.pdf

STRUCTURE AND ORGANIZATION OF CLASSIC "WIDE" DATASETS

Now that we have learned the basics of R/RStudio, we will cover some of the important features of the data, including the structure of the dataset, which can be either wide or long. A wide dataset is organized in a way that a row of responses will be associated with a single participant (respondent). If there are repeated measures for the participant, they will be in separate columns. For example, if a participant were asked their age, gender, birth state, how many hours they slept for three nights in a row, and employment status, the responses would look something like Figure 2.1. Notice that the repeated measures of number of hours slept are in individual columns, and that the respondents—with a respondent identification number—each have their own row. The alternative structure of a dataset can be seen in a long dataset. This is when repeated measures are listed in the rows instead of across the columns. This results in multiple rows for a single participant, thus causing the physical structure of the dataset to be longer. The same data seen in Figure 2.1 as a wide dataset is shown in Figure 2.2; however, the figure is shortened to only show 10 of the 21 entries that existed.

FIGURE 2.1 ● SCREENSHOT OF DATA FROM A <u>WIDE</u> DATASET STRUCTURE

	ID.	age	Sex	Born	Sleep1	Sleep2	Sleep3	Employ
1	129	29	M	AZ	7.5	6.7	9.1	Full
2	347	49	M	NC	6.7	8.3	9.9	Part
3	751	18	F	CA	9.5	7.8	7.7	Student
4	184	57	M	DC	11.2	10.1	9.0	Retired
5	296	41	F	LA	5.6	8.5	10.3	Full
6	48	36	F	PA	7.6	9.3	7.8	Home
7	367	33	M	MA	9.0	8.2	9.0	Full

WideDataSet × | Untitled1 × | Untitled2 × | Untitled3 × | Chapter 11.R ×
Filter

FIGURE 2.2 ● SCREENSHOT OF PARTIAL DATA FROM A <u>LONG</u> DATASET STRUCTURE

WideDataSet × | Untitled1 × | Untitled2 × | Untitled3 × | Cha
Filter

	ID.	age	Sex	Born	Sleep	Day	Employ
1	129	29	M	AZ	7.5	Day 1	Full
2	129	29	M	AZ	6.7	Day 2	Full
3	129	29	M	AZ	9.1	Day 3	Full
4	347	49	M	NC	6.7	Day 1	Part
5	347	49	M	NC	8.3	Day 2	Part
6	347	49	M	NC	7.8	Day 3	Part
7	751	18	F	CA	9.5	Day 1	Student
8	751	18	F	CA	7.8	Day 2	Student
9	751	18	F	CA	7.7	Day 3	Student
10	184	57	M	DC	11.2	Day 1	Retired

Please note that the unit of analysis and distribution of the data change depending on the structure of the data. For instance, if we were to consider the distribution for hours of sleep in the wide dataset, each day would have its own column of values. However, in the long dataset, the distribution would display each measure of hours of sleep as separate rows repeated for the same individual.

We will be working with a wide dataset throughout this book. However, it is important to know what structure of dataset you are working on since statistical procedures will differ for each type. It is also important to have a clear understanding of your units of analysis, distributions, and how they are derived from the dataset with which you are working.

THE *GENERAL SOCIAL SURVEY*

The GSS (Smith et al., 2019) has typically been administered biennially (every two years) since 1972. The survey collects data on Americans' demographics, behaviors, and attitudes. These data can be used by social scientists to provide cross-sectional or "snapshot" observations of social trends that represent the population. In order to become familiar with and obtain data from the GSS, it is as easy as doing an Internet search for the "general social survey" or go to gss.norc.org.

The survey is conducted through face-to-face interviews with participants over 18 years old and takes roughly 90 minutes. Since 2006, the GSS has been conducted in Spanish as well as English. The sampling has changed from its earlier years of modified probability sampling to the more current full probability sampling (see the GSS Codebook). Additionally, the research team aims to reach a representative population by sampling in both rural and urban geographical units.

The full dataset for the GSS has over 950+ variables that are responses to questions about respondents' demographics, such as age, race, income, and marital status, as well as the respondents' feelings about social matters such as Internet use, national politics, and other personal preferences. It is possible to download all years or specific years, but for the purpose of this book, we will be working with the provided subset of 208 variables from 2016. This gives us more than enough data to become familiar with using R/RStudio and navigating the GSS for research purposes. However, at the website (gss.norc.org), click on the tab for "Get the Data" and you can acquire much more than the subset of data we use in this book.

Since we will be working with the data in R/RStudio, it is best for the data to be saved as a "comma separated values" or CSV file, which can be uploaded into R/RStudio pretty easily.

> **Tip:** While working through this book, we recommend having a folder on your desktop titled *CSV* (or something else) for the storage of all your files. This will be convenient for loading your data into R/RStudio when you want to practice. You will be able to set the same working directory for your projects **(setwd('C:/users/username/Desktop/CSV')** because they will be in this folder. Just be sure the code has *your* filepath and working directory information to access the correct file.

The first thing we want to do after saving the GSS data to a CSV file is to open our working directory, followed by uploading the CSV document using the **read.csv** command. After this is completed and the CSV file appears in the environment window, you can consider if you are ready to open any libraries, or just begin analysis and load any libraries as they are needed.

```
setwd('C:/Users/username/Desktop/CSV')# Setting the working
directory.
GSS2016 <- read.csv('GSS2016.csv', header=TRUE)  # Uploading the
CSV file of the data.
```

If the packages for the libraries have already been installed in the RStudio program on the computer you are working on, then the libraries will open with the command **library(libraryname)**. If the packages have not already been installed, then they need to be installed, and the opening of the library re-run.

> **Tip:** To install a package go to the lower right window of RStudio (the viewer window) and click on the Packages tab. Select Install and a new window will appear (Figure 2.3).

FIGURE 2.3 ● WHERE TO FIND "PACKAGES" AND "INSTALL"

Files	Plots	Packages	Help	Viewer			
Install	Update						
	Name		Description			Version	
User Library							
	acepack		ACE and AVAS for Selecting Multiple Regression Transformations			1.4.1	
	assertthat		Easy Pre and Post Assertions			0.2.0	

The install packages window will open in the center of all four RStudio windows. Start typing the package you need in the empty packages bar and RStudio will start to generate possibilities for you to choose. Select the one you want and click on Install (Figure 2.4). Next, go back to the script window and re-run the library.

FIGURE 2.4 ● THE SCREENS FOR INSTALLING PACKAGES

After the working directory is set, the dataset is loaded, and the libraries installed, it is time to start becoming familiar with the data. By looking at the environment window, we can see that there are 208 variables and 2867 respondents. This is where we can double-check that our data has been loaded correctly into the program. After establishing that our data and our RStudio is set up properly, we can begin some data work. For the rest of this book, we will be performing all analyses on this subset of data from the GSS survey.

> **Tip:** It is always a good idea to look at the dataset after you have loaded it into R/RStudio to make sure your values and labels are there. Double-check that you are about to work with the dataset you anticipated, and that it has loaded correctly. You can do this by clicking on the dataset in the environment window and it will appear in the console (Figures 2.5 and 2.6).

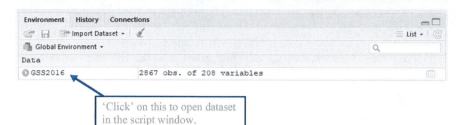

FIGURE 2.5 ●   SCREENSHOT OF THE ENVIRONMENT WINDOW SHOWING THE DATASET HAS BEEN UPLOADED

Environment	History	Connections					
📤 💾 📥 Import Dataset ▾ 🧹						≡ List ▾	⟳
🟦 Global Environment ▾					🔍		
Data							
⊙ GSS2016		2867 obs. of 208 variables					🔲

'Click' on this to open dataset in the script window.

FIGURE 2.6 ●   SCREENSHOT OF THE SCRIPT WINDOW SHOWING THE ACTUAL VALUES (SPREADSHEET) OF THE DATASET

idnum	age	cohort	sex	race	sexornt	born	sibs	agekdbrn	childs	chldidel	marital
155	58	1958	1	1	3	1	4	20	1	-1	1
156	31	1985	1	1	0	1	1	0	0	2	5
157	52	1964	2	3	3	2	11	31	2	-1	1
158	46	1970	2	1	0	2	6	32	2	2	1
159	25	1991	2	1	3	1	2	23	1	4	1
160	54	1962	1	3	0	1	11	20	4	3	2
161	33	1983	2	3	3	2	2	26	1	3	3
162	33	1983	1	3	0	2	2	30	1	2	1
163	61	1955	2	1	3	1	1	19	2	-1	3
164	65	1951	2	1	0	9	13	27	4	3	2
165	53	1963	2	1	0	2	4	0	0	2	5
166	66	1950	2	3	0	2	11	20	8	2	2
167	41	1975	2	1	3	1	2	22	2	-1	5
168	57	1959	2	1	3	1	3	22	2	8	3
169	50	1966	1	2	1	1	1	0	0	-1	5
170	75	1941	1	2	0	1	5	98	4	-1	1

When using GSS data, keep in mind that there are different ways that it can be loaded into R (e.g., through Stata or SPSS) that may require you to alter a script slightly from what you have learned here. Also, be sure to pay attention to spacing and capitalization because R is sensitive to cases and spacing.

VARIABLES AND MEASUREMENT

In statistics, we are often looking to see if there is a relationship between variables beyond what we would see due to chance. These variables can be independent variables, dependent variables, or control variables depending on the statistical analysis chosen to address the research question.

An independent variable (IV), also known as the X variable, is the variable in which its responses are independent of the dependent variable. The IV can be manipulated (or controlled) by the researcher. Whereas, the dependent variable (DV), also known as the Y variable is presumed to be dependent upon the independent variable. We often hypothesize that a dependent variable will change in response to a change in the independent variable. In other words, Y relies on—or responds to—X. Control variables are the variables that we, the researchers, hold constant in order to attempt to isolate the relationship between the IV and the DV.

The level of measurement for variables can be nominal, ordinal, interval, or ratio, depending on how the data are collected for each variable. Nominal and ordinal measurements both have categorical (or discreet) data attributes, while interval and ratio measures are referred to as continuous.

Nominal data can only fit into one classification and the categories are not ranked, not ordered, and not equidistant from each other. Ordinal data fit into one category but the categories *can* be ranked or ordered. Interval and ratio data are both continuous data that have responses that have measurable, equal distances between the (numeric) attributes. Interval data does not have a meaningful zero, and ratio data does have a meaningful zero. A meaningful zero is such that if the response is zero, it represents an absence or lack of something.

Nominal data examples include individuals' political party, marital status, or yes/no options. Ordinal data examples include grade level (freshman, sophomore, junior, senior); 1st, 2nd, and 3rd places; or Likert scales (i.e., strongly agree, agree, neutral, disagree, strongly disagree). Interval data examples include degrees Celsius, year of birth, or IQ. Ratio data examples can include weight, length of time at a job, or number of children. For most of the analyses in this book, we will refer to interval and ratio variables together (i.e., interval/ratio variables).

It is extremely important to remember that the level of measurement is based on how the data are collected. For example, if we wanted to identify the level of measurement for age based on information from a survey, it would depend on how the question was asked. If respondents answered the question, "Are you over the age of 30?" with a yes or a no, the data reflect a dichotomous, or binary, nominal measure of age. If participants answered the question, "How old are you?" by picking from the following ordered options: 18.0–29.9 years old, 30.0–39.9 years old, 40.0–49.9 years old, 50.0–59.9 years old, and 60.0-plus years old, we would consider the data ordinal. If the participants were to respond to the question, "How many years old are you?" by filling in their age in years, that would be interval/ratio data.

When working with the GSS dataset, remember to use the codebook to help inform you of what each code (number) represents. Please do not let the size of the codebook intimidate you; a search of any term (using a Control + F) can get you quickly to the variable you are interested in finding. For a small example of some of the variables we will be working with throughout the following chapters, see Table 2.1. We can also see that our subset of the GSS data contains a range of different levels of variable measurement.

TABLE 2.1 ● LEVELS OF MEASUREMENT FOR VARIABLES IN GSS 2016 SAMPLE EXAMPLES		
Nominal	Ordinal	Interval/Ratio
Race	Degree	Education
Gender	Happiness level	Number of siblings

RECODING VARIABLES

Categorical variables (i.e., nominal, ordinal) have attributes, or categories, that are often represented by a numeric code for statistical analyses. These include variables with only two options (e.g., yes/no), which are special cases known as binary, or dichotomous, variables. Continuous variables (i.e., interval/ratio) are already represented by numeric values (e.g., age).

LOGIC OF CODING

Coding data is the process by which we apply a (typically) numeric code to raw data so that we can enter it into a computer program and run statistical analysis. An example of this is the variable for gender (sex), which has the attributes for male and female. Because this book is using the GSS2016 dataset, the codes have already been established and can be found in the GSS codebook. The code for male is 1 and the code for female is 2. If you are collecting your own data, you, as the researcher, will be the one to establish the codes for your data and the code for male could just as easily be 13 and female 99—they are just numerical representations of the attributes male and female.

When running analyses, we work with the numeric representation of the variable attributes and apply the value labels which are character based (also known as factor or string data). However, when working with many other datasets, or a dataset you have created on your own, you will need to create your own codes for your variable attributes. Just as an example, we will add the value labels to the variable gender (sex) in order to create the output for both the codes and the labels.

```
table(GSS2016$sex)  # Generate a table with raw frequencies for gender.
```

This will be the first (top) output below.

```
GSS2016$sex <- factor(GSS2016$sex,
                      levels = c(1,2),
                      labels = c("Male", "Female"))  #Recode the
value labels for attributes in the variable gender.
```

```
table(GSS2016$sex)
```
Generate a table with count for sex attributes after adding value labels and changing variable to factor.

Outputs: Raw Frequencies for **sex** with codes and with value labels.

1 2 ← *These are the **codes** for the attributes Male and Female*	
1276 1591	

Male Female ← *These are the **value labels** for the attributes Male and Female*	
1276 1591	

Tip: During the process of adding the value labels, we convert the actual data to characters (factor/string) data, which may compromise future mathematical analysis we want to perform. It is best to do this after we have run our analysis.

✓   **INFORMATION BOX 2.1**
_____

Finding the Structure of the Data

If you are unsure of the structure of the data, you can always find out by running the command for structure (**str**). As an example, we can check the structure before we change the variable sex and after we change the variable sex and we can see the structure change from integer to factor.

```
str(GSS2016$sex)
int [1:2867] 1 1 1 2 2 2 1 2 1 1 . . .
```

```
str(GSS2016$sex)
Factor w/2 levels "Male" , "Female": 1 1 1 2 2 2 1 2 1 1 . . .
```

There are plenty of reasons why a researcher would want to recode some of their data, which is to change the attributes and/or numerical classifications of a variable. For example, they might want to change a continuous variable into a categorical variable, create a dichotomous (or binary) variable from a categorical variable, change original values, aggregate (collapse) data, remove unnecessary data, or handle with missing data, to name a few.

One common reason to recode a variable is that a researcher might want to combine a variable's multiple categories in a way that will result in two categories, also known as a dichotomous, or binary, variable. For instance, if we wanted to run an analysis with the variable health, which has seven categories (Excellent, Good, Fair, Poor, Don't know, No answer, and Not applicable), but only wanted two categories (Good or better and Less than good), we would need to recode the variable.

The first thing we need to do is create a new variable that is a duplicate of the original so we can work with the new variable but retain the original variable (Figure 2.7). This gives us the girth to make a mistake and not damage our original data. It is also important to keep the original variable whenever we collapse or aggregate data in order to retain the most detailed level of information in case we want to work with it again later.

In order to create a new variable, let's run a table on our old data to keep and use as a reference to make sure our new variable is created properly.

```
table(GSS2016$health)
```

Output: Raw frequencies of attributes for variable health before recoding.

```
  0    1    2    3    4 9
979  418  919  430  118 3
```

```
GSS2016$healthFact <-(GSS2016$health)  # Create new (duplicate)
variable.
table(GSS2016$healthFact)
```

> **Tip:** Always take a quick look at either the frequencies, or the variable itself, to double-check that your new variable was created properly. In this case, you would want to run the same command you did on the original to be able to compare information.

Output: Raw frequencies of attributes of our new variable healthFact.

```
  0    1    2    3    4 9
979  418  919  430  118 3
```

After creating the new variable, we can add the value labels to the variable and run a frequency table of the variable with the labels. However, you may have noticed that we named this variable healthFact for health *factor*. This is done to show what will happen if we label variables as factors too soon. If we do this, our data become factors (string or characters), which can sometimes create problems with strict numerical analysis. This is a

FIGURE 2.7   ●   NOTE THE CHANGE IN THE ENVIRONMENT WINDOW FROM 208 VARIABLES TO 209

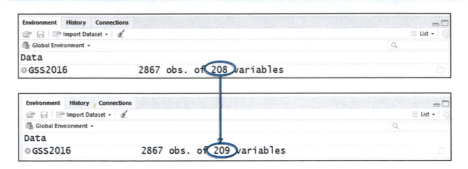

compelling argument for always creating a *new* variable rather than making changes to the original variable.

Before recoding, we need to know what the codes actually represent. We can find this information by using the GSS codebook. This codebook is a very large PDF file that explains all 900+ variables and their attributes. We highly recommend the search function!

✔ INFORMATION BOX 2.2

Searching for a Variable

Using the Control + F shortcut to produce a search window is a quick way to search for a variable. After searching for the health variable, which is what this was created from, you can see the variable attributes and their codes (refer to the screenshot below). As an example, *Fair* health responses were coded as 3.

```
GSS2016$healthFact <-factor(GSS2016$health,
                    levels=c(1,2,3,4,8,9,0),
                    labels=c("Excellent", "Good", "Fair",
                    "Poor", "Don't know", "No answer",
                    "Not applicable"))
table(GSS2016$healthFact)
```

Output: Raw frequencies of attributes of new variable `healthFact` with the labels created.

Excellent	Good	Fair	Poor
418	919	430	118
Don't know	No answer	Not applicable	
0	3	979	

In addition to looking at the frequencies, we can become familiar with all of the raw values by simply running the name of the data and variable with the dollar sign operator discussed earlier:

```
GSS2016$health
```

Output: Screenshot of a portion of the individual responses to the variable health.

```
  [1] 2 0 2 2 1 0 4 2 2 2 0 4 0 2 0 1 1 0 0 2 0 1 0 1 3 0 1 0 0
 [30] 2 0 2 2 3 3 0 0 2 1 0 2 2 0 2 0 3 0 2 1 0 0 1 0 2 1 0 0 0
 [59] 1 2 1 0 3 0 2 3 0 3 3 3 3 2 0 0 1 0 1 2 1 2 2 1 2 2 2 2 0
 [88] 3 2 3 0 3 2 2 2 0 0 0 2 2 2 0 3 1 3 3 2 3 3 3 2 3 1 2 0 0 2
[117] 2 0 2 0 1 1 1 3 0 0 1 2 0 2 0 1 2 4 4 2 0 3 1 2 4 2 3 2 0
[146] 0 2 0 0 2 1 0 2 3 2 1 2 2 0 1 0 2 3 3 0 4 4 0 1 2 0 3 0 1
```

```
GSS2016$healthFact
```

Output: Screenshot of a portion of the individual responses to the variable healthFact.

```
 [1] Good           Not applicable  Good            Good            Excellent
 [6] Not applicable  Poor           Good            Good            Good
[11] Not applicable  Poor           Not applicable  Good            Not applicable
[16] Excellent       Excellent      Not applicable  Not applicable  Good
[21] Not applicable  Excellent      Not applicable  Excellent       Fair
[26] Not applicable  Excellent      Not applicable  Not applicable  Good
[31] Not applicable  Good           Good            Fair            Fair
[36] Not applicable  Not applicable  Good           Excellent       Not applicable
```

We are able to see immediately that the labels have been successfully applied. Also noticeable, from either the frequency outputs or the data boxes, is the large amount of No answer and Not applicable cases. The GSS sometimes skips certain question models for certain individuals. When we recode the data, we will want to account for that and remove these from the calculations. We will be combining the Good and Excellent responses in a single category, "Good or better," which has a code of 1, and Fair and Poor responses into the category "Less than good" to which we will apply the code 2.

When we gave labels to the variable `healthFact` we created the new variable as a factor variable (Figure 2.8). However, we need to have a numeric variable in order to recode, so we will be creating a new variable (`healthBiNom`) that will be a binary nominal variable; meaning it has only two attributes (1 = Good or better, 2 = Less than good).

```
GSS2016$healthBiNom <-(GSS2016$health) # Create new (duplicate)
variable based on the original.
```

FIGURE 2.8 ● NOTE THE CHANGE IN THE ENVIRONMENT WINDOW FROM 209 TO 210

```
table(GSS2016$healthBiNom)
```

Output: Raw frequencies of attributes for variable `healthBiNom` before recoding.

```
   0    1    2    3    4   9
 979  418  919  430  118   3
```

```
GSS2016$healthBiNom
```

Output: Screenshot of a portion of individual responses of `healthBiNom` before recoding.

```
  [1] 2 0 2 2 1 0 4 2 2 2 0 4 0 2 0 1 1 0 0 2 0 1 0 1 3 0 1 0 0
 [30] 2 0 2 2 3 3 0 0 2 1 0 2 2 0 2 0 3 0 2 1 0 0 1 0 2 1 0 0 0
 [59] 1 2 1 0 3 0 2 3 0 3 3 3 3 2 0 0 1 0 1 2 1 2 2 1 2 2 2 2 0
 [88] 3 2 3 0 3 2 2 2 0 0 0 2 2 2 0 3 1 3 3 2 3 3 2 3 1 2 0 0 2
[117] 2 0 2 0 1 1 1 3 0 0 1 2 0 2 0 1 2 4 4 2 0 3 1 2 4 2 3 2 0
[146] 0 2 0 0 2 1 0 2 3 2 1 2 2 0 1 0 2 3 3 0 4 4 0 1 2 0 3 0 1
[175] 0 2 1 3 2 3 3 4 3 0 2 0 1 2 3 0 2 0 2 3 2 0 2 2 2 1 2 0 0
```

Now we will run the scripts for recoding the variable from the original seven possible categories to create only two categories. Then we will examine frequencies and a snapshot of the data to make sure the recoding was successful. After determining that the 8, 9, and 0 codes are representing answers that need to be removed from the analysis, and that the strong positive responses of 1 and 2 (Excellent and Good) will be grouped and the neutral and negative responses of 3 and 4 (Fair and Poor) will be grouped, we will then recode the new variable using the script below.

```
GSS2016$healthBiNom[GSS2016$healthBiNom==0]=NA
GSS2016$healthBiNom[GSS2016$healthBiNom==8]=NA
GSS2016$healthBiNom[GSS2016$healthBiNom==9]=NA
GSS2016$healthBiNom[GSS2016$healthBiNom==1]=1
GSS2016$healthBiNom[GSS2016$healthBiNom==2]=1
GSS2016$healthBiNom[GSS2016$healthBiNom==3]=2
GSS2016$healthBiNom[GSS2016$healthBiNom==4]=2
```

```
GSS2016$healthBiNom
```

Output: Screenshot of a portion of responses to the variable `healthBiNom` after recoding.

```
 [1]    1  NA  1  1  1 NA  2  1  1  1 NA  2  NA 1 NA  1   1 NA NA
 [20]   1  NA  1 NA  1  2  NA 1 NANA 1 NA  1  1  2   2 NA NA  1
 [39]   1  NA  1  1 NA  1  NA 2 NA  1   1 NA NA 1 NA  1   1 NA NA
 [58]  NA  1  1  1 NA  2  NA 1  2 NA  2  2   2  2  1 NA NA  1 NA
 [77]   1  1  1  1  1  1   1  1  1  1 NA  2   1  2 NA  2  1  1  1
 [96]  NA NANA  1  1  1  NA 2  1  2  2  1   2  2  1  2   1  1 NA
[115]  NA  1  1 NA  1 NA   1  1  1  2 NANA  1  1 NA  1 NA  1  1
[134]   2  2  1 NA  2  1   1  2  1  2   1 NA NA 1 NANA  1   1 NA
[153]   1  2  1  1  1  1  NA 1 NA  1  2  2  NA 2  2 NA  1   1 NA
```

```
table(GSS2016$healthBiNom)
```

Output: Raw frequencies of attributes for variable `healthBiNom` after recoding.

```
  1     2
1337  548
```

It is also possible to look at the structure of a variable by using the "str" script with the variable to indicate how the data is being read by R.

```
str(GSS2016$health)
str(GSS2016$healthFact)
str(GSS2016$healthBiNom)
```

Outputs: Structures of the three variables just recoded.

```
 int [1:2867] 2 0 2 2 1 0 4 2 2 2 ...
Factor w/7 levels "Excellent" , "Good": 2 7 2 2 1 7 4 2 2 2 ...
 num [1:2867] 1 NA 1 1 1 NA 2 1 1 1 ...
```

We can then generate a new factor variable that will be a factor variable with value labels for the binary health variable. We will add an *L* to the variable name to remind us that this health variable is the one with the NA and with the labels (Figure 2.9).

```
GSS2016$healthBiNomL <-factor(GSS2016$healthBiNom,
                              levels=c(1,2),
                              labels=c("Good or better", "Less
                              than good"))
```

FIGURE 2.9 ● NOTE THE CHANGE IN THE ENVIRONMENT WINDOW

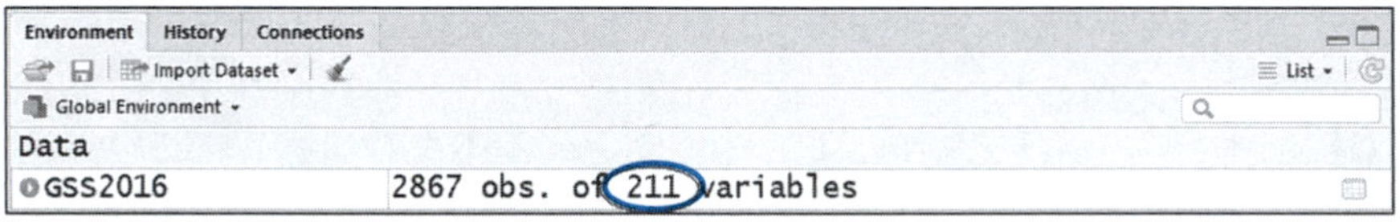

```
GSS2016$healthBiNomL
```

Output: Screenshot of a portion of responses to the variable `healthBiNomL` after recoding.

[1] Good or better	<NA>	Good or better	Good or better	Good or better
[6] <NA>	Less than good	Good or better	Good or better	Good or better
[11] <NA>	Less than good	<NA>	Good or better	<NA>
[16] Good or better	Good or better	<NA>	<NA>	Good or better
[21] <NA>	Good or better	<NA>	Good or better	Less than good
[26] <NA>	Good or better	<NA>	<NA>	Good or better
[31] <NA>	Good or better	Good or better	Less than good	Less than good
[36] <NA>	<NA>	Good or better	Good or better	<NA>
[41] Good or better	Good or better	<NA>	Good or better	<NA>

```
table(GSS2016$healthBiNomL)
```

Output: Raw frequencies of attributes of new variable `healthBiNomL` with the labels created.

Good or better	Less than good
1337	548

Tip: If you click on the data frame in our environment window (for this example it would be GSS2016), you can navigate to the end to see the new variables that have been created (Figures 2.10 and 2.11).

FIGURE 2.10 ● SCREENSHOT OF THE LOCATION OF DATA FRAME AREA IN THE GLOBAL ENVIRONMENT TO BE CLICKED

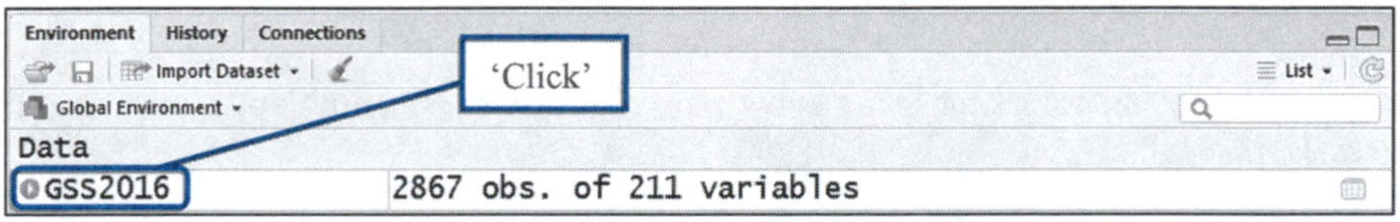

FIGURE 2.11 ● SCREENSHOT OF THE LAST FEW COLUMNS OF DATASET

healthFact	healthBiNom	healthBiNomL
Good	1	Good or better
Not applicable	NA	NA
Good	1	Good or better
Good	1	Good or better
Excellent	1	Good or better
Not applicable	NA	NA
Poor	2	Less than good
Good	1	Good or better
Good	1	Good or better
Good	1	Good or better
Not applicable	NA	NA
Poor	2	Less than good
Not applicable	NA	NA
Good	1	Good or better

We can also recode the variable for respondents' age at which first child was born (agekdbrn) using logical operations. First, we will need to run a table of the variable to see what responses exist.

```
table(GSS2016$agekdbrn)
```

Output: Frequencies of age at which first child was born (agekdbrn).

```
  0    9 12 13 14 15 16 17   18   19   20   21  22  23   24  25  26
797    1  1  4 12 16 67 84  135  165  164  170 115 124  101 144 109

 27 28 29 30 31 32 33 34   35   36   37   38  39  40   41  42  43
 89 76 71 97 50 55 41 31   38   19   18   13  13  15    4   5   2

 44 45 46 47 98 99
  1  3  2  1  3  11
```

We then recode the values for Don't know (98), No Answer (99), and Not applicable (0); to make them all NA.

```
GSS2016$agekdbrnNEW<-GSS2016$agekdbrn
GSS2016$agekdbrnNEW[GSS2016$agekdbrn==0]=NA
GSS2016$agekdbrnNEW[GSS2016$agekdbrn==98]=NA
GSS2016$agekdbrnNEW[GSS2016$agekdbrn==99]=NA

table(GSS2016$agekdbrnNEW)
```

Output: Frequencies of age at which first child was born (agekdbrnNEW) after recoding for NA.

```
  9 12 13 14 15 16  17   18   19  20   21   22   23   24  25   26 27
  1  1  4 12 16 67  84  135  165 164  170  115  124  101 144  109 89

 28 29 30 31 32 33 34   35   36   37  38   39   40   41  42   43 44
 76 71 97 50 55 41 31   38   19   18  13   13   15    4   5    2  1

 45 46 47
  3  2  1
```

Now we can apply some logical operations to recode the variable into three age categories of less than 25, 25 to 35, and Over 35.

```
GSS2016$agekdbrnNEW[GSS2016$agekdbrn>35]= 1
GSS2016$agekdbrnNEW[GSS2016$agekdbrn>= 20 &
GSS2016$agekdbrn<=35]= 2
GSS2016$agekdbrnNEW[GSS2016$agekdbrn<20]= 3

table(GSS2016$agekdbrnNEW)
```

Output: Frequencies of age at which first child was born (agekdbrnNEW) after recoding.

```
   1     2     3
 110  1475  1282
```

We can also create a new variable with value labels by writing the label directly into the script instead of having to write it independently. Here, we create another variable for the participant's age at the birth of their first child and treat it as a categorical/factor variable.

```
GSS2016$agekdbrnNEW2[GSS2016$agekdbrn>35]= "Over 35"
GSS2016$agekdbrnNEW2[GSS2016$agekdbrn>=20 &
GSS2016$agekdbrn<=35]= "25 to 35"
GSS2016$agekdbrnNEW2[GSS2016$agekdbrn<20]= "Less than 25"

table(GSS2016$agekdbrnNEW2)
```

Output: Frequencies of age at which first child was born (agekdbrnNEW2) after recoding.

25 to 35	Less than 25	Over 35
1475	1282	110

Tip: Similar to spreadsheets, it is also possible to see if a variable has been read by RStudio as a factor or as a number by looking at the actual data cases/observations in the script window. When the data in a column is right-side aligned, it is being read as numeric; however, if it is left-side aligned, it is being read as string information.

Output: Screenshot of left- and right-aligned data in the script window.

chldidealNA	chldidealNAL	chldidealNAL2	agekdbrnNEW	agekdbrnNEW2
3	3	3 children	2	25 to 35
2	2	2 children	3	Less than 25
NA	NA	NA	2	25 to 35
2	2	2 children	3	Less than 25
NA	NA	NA	2	25 to 35
2	2	2 children	2	25 to 35
3	3	3 children	2	25 to 35
NA	NA	NA	3	Less than 25
8	As many as you want	As many as you want	3	Less than 25
NA	NA	NA	2	25 to 35
4	4	4 children	3	Less than 25
3	3	3 children	3	Less than 25
8	As many as you want	As many as you want	2	25 to 35
NA	NA	NA	3	Less than 25
2	2	2 children	2	25 to 35
NA	NA	NA	2	25 to 35
NA	NA	NA	2	25 to 35
2	2	2 children	3	Less than 25

Another reason to recode a variable is to remove any negative numbers that may be included in the coding—for example, to change some missing values (e.g., -999) into truly missing values (i.e., NA). This can influence statistical analysis. As an example, we can look at the variable `chldidel`, which includes the responses to the question, "What do you think is the ideal number of children for a family to have?" Table 2.2 shows how the variable is originally coded. If we do not recode the value 9 to missing, then statistical analyses will be run as though those individuals would like to have nine children instead of their actual response, "No Answer/Don't Know." The following steps will take you through the recoding process.

TABLE 2.2 ● THE GSS CODES FOR VARIABLE `chldidel`	
Original code	**Label**
0	None
1	One
2	Two
3	Three
4	Four
5	Five
6	Six
7	Seven or more
8	As many as you want
9	No answer, don't know
-1	Not applicable

```
table(GSS2016$chldidel)
```

Output: Raw frequencies of attributes of new variable `chldidel`.

```
 -1   0   1   2   3   4   5  6   7   8
980  13  36 844 477 194  35  6  11 271
```

```
GSS2016$chldidealNA <-(GSS2016$chldidel)
```
Create new (duplicate) variable
```
table(GSS2016$chldidealNA)
```

Output: Raw frequencies of attributes of new variable `chldidealNA`.

-1	0	1	2	3	4	5	6	7	8
980	13	36	844	477	194	35	6	11	271

```
GSS2016$chldidealNA[GSS2016$chldidealNA=="-1"]=NA
GSS2016$chldidealNA[GSS2016$chldidealNA==9]=NA

table(GSS2016$chldidealNA)
```

Output: Raw frequencies of attributes of new variable `chldidealNA` after recoding.

0	1	2	3	4	5	6	7	8
13	36	844	477	194	35	6	11	271

```
GSS2016$chldidealNA
```

Output: Screenshot of a portion of responses to the variable `chldidealNA` after recoding.

```
  [1]   3  2 NA 2 NA 2  3  NA  8 NA 4   3   8 NA 2  NA NA 2  2   3  3NA 2
 [24] NA NA  4  3  3  2 NA  2  NA 3 NA 2   2  2   4 NA  3 NA 2   2 NA2 NA
 [47]  2  2 NA 8  2  2  3 NA  4  3  3   2 NA 4 NA  5 NA 8  2 NA 3  5   2
 [70]  2  3  4  3  5  8  2   2  3 NA NA 2 NA 2 NA NA  2  8  2 NA NA2 NA
 [93]  2 NA NA 2  2  2 NA NA NA 2   2 NA NA 4 NA  3   2 NA 2 NA 3  3   8
[116] NA NA  3 NA 2  2 NA NA 2  2  3   3 NA 2   2  4   3 NA 2 NA 2  2 NA
```

We can then create a new variable that is a factor variable of the labels for the number of ideal children after the recoding of the missing data.

```
GSS2016$chldidealNAL <-factor(GSS2016$chldidealNA,
levels=c(0,1,2,3,4,5,6,7,8),
labels=c("No children", "1 child",
                "2 children" , "3 children" , "4 children",
                "5 children" , "6 children" , "7 or more",
                "As many as you want"))
table(GSS2016$chldidealNAL)
```

Output: Raw frequencies of attributes of new variable `chldidealNAL` after recoding.

No children	1 child	2 children	3 children	4 children
13	36	844	477	194
5 children	6 children	7 or more	As many as you want	
35	6	11	271	

Table 2.3 highlights the changes made from the codes for the variable `chldidealNA` to the new codes for variable `chldidealNAL`, which includes the labels and has changed the no answer, don't know to a true missing response: `NA`. This was done in order to remove the -1 and 9 codes so that they are not included as meaningful answers in statistical calculations.

TABLE 2.3 ● THE GSS CODES FOR VARIABLE `chldidealNA` OR `chldidealNAL`			
Original Code	**Label**	**New Code**	**New Label**
0	None	0	No children
1	One	1	1 child
2	Two	2	2 children
3	Three	3	3 children
4	Four	4	4 children
5	Five	5	5 children
6	Six	6	6 children
7	Seven or more	7	Seven or more
8	As many as you want	8	As many as you want
9	No answer, Don't know	NA	Not applicable
-1	Not Applicable	NA	Not applicable

In Chapters 3 and 4, you will learn different ways to generate descriptive statistics for your data. As with many operations in R and RStudio, there are several different ways to do this. However, one way to validate that your data recoding was successful is to run some descriptive statistics before and after to ensure the recoding did in fact take place. The following example uses the library package **pastecs** to produce descriptive statistics for comparisons on continuous variables. In order to run the **stat.desc** command you need to first open the `library (pastecs)`.

```
library(pastecs)  # Be sure to open the library for pastecs.
stat.desc(GSS2016$chldidealNA)  # Running descriptive statistics.
```

Output: Descriptive statistics for variable `childidealNA`.

```
    nbr.val       nbr.null        nbr.na           min           max          range
1.887000e+03 1.300000e+01 9.800000e+02 0.000000e+00 8.000000e+00 8.000000e+00
     sum         median          mean       SE.mean    CI.mean.0.95      var
6.387000e+03 3.000000e+00 3.384738e+00 4.789750e-02 9.393765e-02 4.329099e+00
    std.dev       coef.var
2.080649e+00 6.147149e-01
```

RECODING MISSING VALUES

There are entire books written on the topic of handling missing data. For the purpose of this book, most of the values of "Don't know," "No answer," or "Not applicable" will be converted to the value NA, which is understood by R to mean "truly missing." Sometimes when working with large datasets, a researcher may decide to recode missing responses in the entire dataset prior to working with it, and not each time they run a calculation. There are a variety of other procedures for handling missing data but we will not discuss those in this book.

If we are using a dataset that has already been coded, such as the GSS, and we simply need to recode a value as missing, we can do so by recoding the value so that it is interpreted by R as "truly missing" (NA) and thus not included in any calculations. For example, the codes for the variable zodiac include 1 through 12, each of which corresponds to one of the twelve astrological signs of the zodiac—but also "98" and "99". Based on information in the codebook, we know that the latter two numbers represent "Don't know," and "No answer," respectively. Accordingly, we need to recode the "98" and "99" values to NA so that they are not calculated as meaningful responses in statistical analyses. First, create a new variable and name it zodiac2.

```
GSS2016$zodiac2<-(GSS2016$zodiac)  # Creating new variable.
table(GSS2016$zodiac2)  # Observing frequencies of categories.
```

Output: Raw frequencies of attributes of new variable zodiac2 before recoding.

1	2	3	4	5	6	7	8	9	10	11	12	98	99
225	240	224	257	235	274	227	219	214	197	236	234	5	80

```
GSS2016$zodiac2[GSS2016$zodiac2==98]=NA  # Recoding the missing
values as NA.
GSS2016$zodiac2[GSS2016$zodiac2==99]=NA
table(GSS2016$zodiac2) # Observing frequencies after recoding.
```

Output: Raw frequencies of attributes of new variable `zodiac2` after recoding.

1	2	3	4	5	6	7	8	9	10	11	12
225	240	224	257	235	274	227	219	214	197	236	234

There are other ways to handle missing values that will depend on the data you are working with. In order to understand missing values a little better, we will start off with a simple example. Open a spreadsheet (e.g., Excel) and input the data exactly as it appears in Table 2.4. Title the spreadsheet "NotApp" and save it in your desktop folder.

Now we will open RStudio and load in the CSV file. Name the dataset "NOT".

If you loaded the "NOT" file into the same folder as the one you are currently working in, you do not need to set the working directory a second time.

```
setwd('C:/Users/username/Desktop/CSV') # Setting the working
directory (In this code, the CSV file is saved in a desktop folder called
CSV).
```

TABLE 2.4 ● DATA TO BE COPIED INTO A SPREADSHEET AND USED FOR THE NEXT EXAMPLE

	A	B
1	ABC	XYZ
2	1	7
3	2	2
4	4	4
5	6	8
6	NA	4
7	8	1
8	4	2
9	8	NA
10	4	6
11	2	3
12	1	4
13	8	9
14	0	3
15	5	2
16	NA	0
17	6	0

```
NOT <- read.csv('NotApp.csv',
header=TRUE) # Reading in the CSV file
NotApp and calling it NOT.
```

Next we can identify the cases in the variable ABC, and in the variable XYZ that are NA:

```
is.na(NOT$ABC)
is.na(NOT$XYZ)
```

Outputs: Showing where the NA is TRUE for `ABC` and `XYZ` independently.

```
> is.na(NOT$ABC)
 [1] FALSE FALSE FALSE FALSE TRUE
     FALSE FALSE FALSE FALSE FALSE
[11] FALSE FALSE FALSE FALSE TRUE
     FALSE
> is.na(NOT$XYZ)
 [1] FALSE FALSE FALSE FALSE FALSE
     FALSE FALSE TRUE FALSE FALSE
[11] FALSE FALSE FALSE FALSE FALSE
     FALSE
```

```
is.na(NOT)
```

Output: Showing where "is NA" is TRUE for the dataset NOT.

```
         ABC    XYZ
  [1,]  FALSE  FALSE
  [2,]  FALSE  FALSE
  [3,]  FALSE  FALSE
  [4,]  FALSE  FALSE
  [5,]   TRUE  FALSE
  [6,]  FALSE  FALSE
  [7,]  FALSE  FALSE
  [8,]  FALSE   TRUE
  [9,]  FALSE  FALSE
 [10,]  FALSE  FALSE
 [11,]  FALSE  FALSE
 [12,]  FALSE  FALSE
 [13,]  FALSE  FALSE
 [14,]  FALSE  FALSE
 [15,]   TRUE  FALSE
 [16,]  FALSE  FALSE
```

If we add an exclamation point (!), this is the equivalent of indicating "is not". The following script indicates that all the values that are not NA should be considered TRUE.

```
!is.na(NOT)
```

Output: Showing where "is not NA" is TRUE for the dataset NOT.

```
         ABC    XYZ
  [1,]   TRUE   TRUE
  [2,]   TRUE   TRUE
  [3,]   TRUE   TRUE
  [4,]   TRUE   TRUE
  [5,]  FALSE   TRUE
  [6,]   TRUE   TRUE
  [7,]   TRUE   TRUE
  [8,]   TRUE  FALSE
  [9,]   TRUE   TRUE
 [10,]   TRUE   TRUE
 [11,]   TRUE   TRUE
```

```
[12,]   TRUE   TRUE
[13,]   TRUE   TRUE
[14,]   TRUE   TRUE
[15,]   FALSE  TRUE
[16,]   TRUE   TRUE
```

It is possible to remove the NAs from the dataset by using the **na.omit** command (Figure 2.12). This will remove the data for the entire row that contains the NA.

```
na.omit(NOT)
```

FIGURE 2.12 ● COMPARISON OF OUTPUT AFTER OMITTING NA DATA AND ORIGINAL DATA VALUES FOR NOT

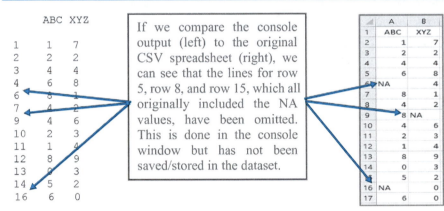

We can create a new dataset with all of the rows with NA omitted (Figure 2.13).

```
newOMIT<-na.omit(NOT)
```

> **Tip:** Keep in mind that eliminating all rows with missing values often removes many cases (and a great deal of additional data) so this practice is generally not advisable.

If we keep the NA cases in the data, which is preferred, then we use the **na.pass** command to ignore the NA cases without removing them from the dataset entirely. For example, if we wanted to compute a new variable (`multiplied`) of ABC multiplied with XYZ, we can tell R to compute the variables while passing over the NA responses (Figure 2.14, p. 50).

```
NOT$multiplied<-na.pass(NOT$ABC*NOT$XYZ)
```

R will not run some calculations (e.g., finding the mean) unless it has been told to remove the NA cases from its calculations. In order to remove the missing values from the calculations,

FIGURE 2.13 ● SCREENSHOTS OF THE NEW DATA FRAME WITHOUT THE
NA CASES

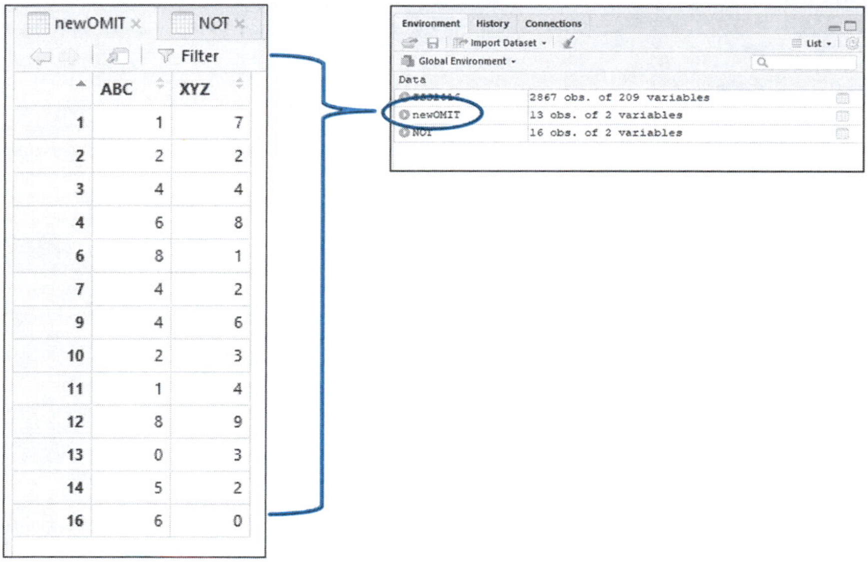

use the `na.rm = TRUE` script. Let's try it both ways to compare the different output. It is clear that without removing the NA cases, R will not calculate the mean properly. The **na.rm** command can be used in other calculations as well.

```
mean(NOT$ABC)
mean(NOT$ABC, na.rm = TRUE)
```

Outputs: Mean of the ABC variable with and without the NA cases.

```
> mean(NOT$ABC)
[1] NA
> mean(NOT$ABC, na.rm = TRUE)
[1] 4.214286
```

Imputation

If you are interested in imputation or inputting a value in place of the NA instead of removing the NA, that can be done, too. For instance, if you have the mean or median of the variable you can impute that instead of the missing value. Let's try imputation with the `multiplied` variable. There are three different ways to go about getting the mean and median. The first is by removing the NA values; the second is by calling only the data that is not an NA value, using the "is not NA" command (**!is.na**); and the third is by using the package **pastecs**.

FIGURE 2.14 ● SCREENSHOT OF THE NEW VARIABLE COMPUTED (multiplied) USING THE NA.PASS

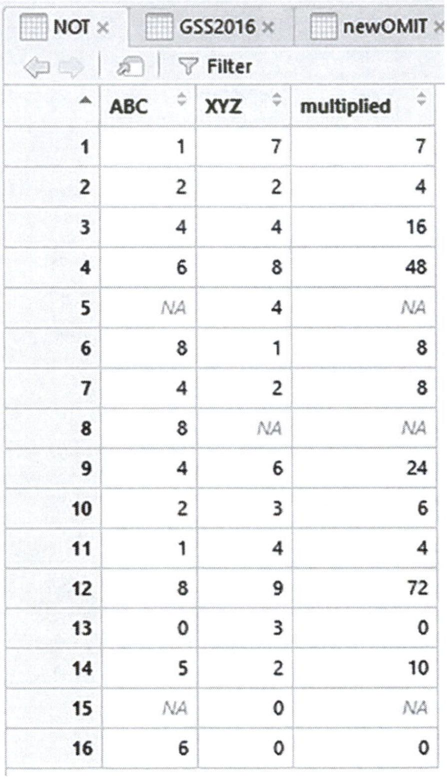

	ABC	XYZ	multiplied
1	1	7	7
2	2	2	4
3	4	4	16
4	6	8	48
5	NA	4	NA
6	8	1	8
7	4	2	8
8	8	NA	NA
9	4	6	24
10	2	3	6
11	1	4	4
12	8	9	72
13	0	3	0
14	5	2	10
15	NA	0	NA
16	6	0	0

```
mean(NOT$multiplied, na.rm = TRUE)
median(NOT$multiplied, na.rm = TRUE)
sd(NOT$multiplied, na.rm = TRUE) # Whenever you are obtaining a
```
mean value, it is always a good idea to get the standard deviation as well.

Outputs: Mean, median, and standard deviation of the multiplied variable using na.rm.

```
> mean(NOT$multiplied, na.rm = TRUE)
[1] 15.92308
> median(NOT$multiplied, na.rm = TRUE)
[1] 8
> sd(NOT$multiplied, na.rm = TRUE)
[1] 21.15207
```

```
mean(NOT$multiplied[!is.na(NOT$multiplied)])
median(NOT$multiplied[!is.na(NOT$multiplied)])
sd(NOT$multiplied[!is.na(NOT$multiplied)])
```

Outputs: Mean, median, and standard deviation of the `multiplied` variable using `!is.na`.

```
> mean(NOT$multiplied[!is.na(NOT$multiplied)])
[1] 15.92308
> median(NOT$multiplied[!is.na(NOT$multiplied)])
[1] 8
> sd(NOT$multiplied[!is.na(NOT$multiplied)])
[1] 21.15207
```

And the third is by using a command from the **pastecs** library: **stat.desc**.

```
library(pastecs)  # You need to make sure you opened the package
and loaded the library for "pastecs" (this can take a minute or two).
stat.desc(NOT$multiplied)
```

Outputs: Descriptive statistics for the multiplied variable using stat.desc.

nbr.val	nbr.null	nbr.na	min	max
13.000000	2.000000	3.000000	0.000000	72.000000

range	sum	median	mean	SE.mean
72.000000	207.000000	8.000000	15.923077	5.866530

CI.mean.0.95	var	std.dev	coef.var
12.782071	447.410256	21.152075	1.328391

After obtaining the mean and median values for the variable, it is best to create a new second variable to work with. In this book, we have created two new variables `mult1` and `mult2` so that we can perform a mean imputation and a median imputation.

```
NOT$mult1<-NOT$multiplied
NOT$mult2<-NOT$multiplied

NOT$mult1[is.na(NOT$mult1)]<-mean(NOT$multiplied[!is.
na(NOT$multiplied)]) # Mean imputation
```

Output: The mean imputation for `mult1` using the `!is.na` command.

	ABC	XYZ	multiplied	mult1	mult2
1	1	7	7	7.00000	7
2	2	2	4	4.00000	4
3	4	4	16	16.00000	16
4	6	8	48	48.00000	48
5	NA	4	NA	15.92308	NA
6	8	1	8	8.00000	8
7	4	2	8	8.00000	8
8	8	NA	NA	15.92308	NA
9	4	6	24	24.00000	24
10	2	3	6	6.00000	6
11	1	4	4	4.00000	4
12	8	9	72	72.00000	72
13	0	3	0	0.00000	0
14	5	2	10	10.00000	10
15	NA	0	NA	15.92308	NA
16	6	0	0	0.00000	0

```
NOT$mult2[is.na(NOT$mult2)]<-median(NOT$multiplied, na.rm =
TRUE)  # Median imputation
```

Output: The median imputation for `mult2` using the `na.rm` command.

	ABC	XYZ	multiplied	mult1	mult2
1	1	7	7	7.00000	7
2	2	2	4	4.00000	4
3	4	4	16	16.00000	16
4	6	8	48	48.00000	48
5	NA	4	NA	15.92308	8
6	8	1	8	8.00000	8
7	4	2	8	8.00000	8
8	8	NA	NA	15.92308	8
9	4	6	24	24.00000	24
10	2	3	6	6.00000	6
11	1	4	4	4.00000	4
12	8	9	72	72.00000	72
13	0	3	0	0.00000	0
14	5	2	10	10.00000	10
15	NA	0	NA	15.92308	8
16	6	0	0	0.00000	0

```
stat.desc(NOT$mult1)
```

Outputs: Descriptive statistics for `mult1` after mean imputation.

nbr.val	nbr.null	nbr.na	min	max
16.000000	2.000000	0.000000	0.000000	72.000000

range	sum	median	mean	SE.mean
72.000000	254.769231	9.000000	15.923077	4.729748

CI.mean.0.95	var	std.dev	coef.var
10.081218	357.928205	18.918991	1.188149

If we compare the two descriptive statistics from before and after the mean imputation, we see that the number of observations has increased from 13 to 16, which makes sense because we imputed values where there used to be NAs for three cases. That means three additional observations are now in the data. The mean has remained the same as before the imputation because we used the mean as the value for imputation.

COMPUTING VARIABLES

Computing variables is the process in which we use (an) existing variable(s) with a mathematical operation that result(s) in a new variable.

For example, if we wanted to create a measure of the total years of education for a participant's mother (`maeduc`) and father (`paeduc`) combined, we would compute a new variable with this information. The first thing that needs to be done is to recode the data to remove the "not applicable" (97), "don't know" (98), "no answer" (99) cases for both variables.

```
table(GSS2016$maeduc)
```

Output: Frequencies of responses for `maeduc` before coding for NA.

0	1	2	3	4	5	6	7	8	9	10	11
59	5	11	27	16	32	77	29	182	61	98	86

12	13	14	15	16	17	18	19	20	97	98	99
1055	100	236	53	302	20	89	10	33	101	180	5

```
table(GSS2016$paeduc)
```

Output: Frequencies of responses for `paeduc` before coding for NA.

0	1	2	3	4	5	6	7	8	9	10	11	12	13	14	15
43	8	11	40	26	24	80	32	157	60	74	65	774	72	147	35

16	17	18	19	20	97	98	99
274	28	67	16	59	550	221	4

```
GSS2016$maeduc[GSS2016$maeduc==97]=NA
GSS2016$maeduc[GSS2016$maeduc==98]=NA
GSS2016$maeduc[GSS2016$maeduc==99]=NA

GSS2016$paeduc[GSS2016$paeduc==97]=NA
GSS2016$paeduc[GSS2016$paeduc==98]=NA
GSS2016$paeduc[GSS2016$paeduc==99]=NA

table(GSS2016$maeduc)
```

Output: Frequencies of responses for `maeduc` after coding for NA.

0	1	2	3	4	5	6	7	8	9	10	11	12	13
59	5	11	27	16	32	77	29	182	61	98	86	1055	100

14	15	16	17	18	19	20
236	53	302	20	89	10	33

```
table(GSS2016$paeduc)
```

Output: Frequencies of responses for **paeduc** after coding for NA.

0	1	2	3	4	5	6	7	8	9	10	11	12	13	14	15	16
43	8	11	40	26	24	80	32	157	60	74	65	774	72	147	35	274

17	18	19	20
28	67	16	59

Next, we simultaneously create a new variable for parent education (`parentEDUC`) and compute the data for the variable by adding the data from highest year of school completed by the mother (`maeduc`) to the data from highest year of school completed by the father (`paeduc`) (Figure 2.15). Because both variables have a range of 20 with 0 as the minimum and 20 as the maximum, it is anticipated that the newly computed variable range cannot exceed 40 with a minimum of 0 and a maximum of 40. We can follow the computation of the variable with a frequency table to see if that is true.

FIGURE 2.15 ● SCREENSHOTS OF THE INDIVIDUAL VARIABLES (maeduc AND paeduc) THAT WERE ADDED TOGETHER TO COMPUTE THE NEW VARIABLE (ParentEDUC)

paeduc	maeduc		ParentEDUC
18	13		31
8	12		20
12	8		20
NA	12		NA
16	12		28
11	12		23
12	12		24
5	5		10
8	8		16
14	15		29
12	13		25
12	NA		NA
NA	NA		NA
NA	NA		NA
NA	NA		NA
12	NA		NA
5	8		13

paeduc + maeduc = ParentEDUC

```
GSS2016$ParentEDUC<-(GSS2016$paeduc+GSS2016$maeduc)
table(GSS2016$ParentEDUC)
```

Output: Frequencies of responses for combined highest years of education (parentEDUC).

```
 0  1  2  3  4  5  6   7  8  9  10 11  12 13 14 15 16
23  2  6  8  5  3 15   4 13    10 12 13  42  9 31 18 68


17 18 19 20 21 22 23   24 25 26  27 28  29 30 31 32 33
24 44 24 87 45 82 61  464 75 141 53 157 42 92 18 115 22


34 35 36 37 38 39 40
43  7 39 10 15  3  8
```

REMOVING OUTLIERS

An outlier is an extreme or unusual value within a variable which typically exists in continuous (interval/ratio) data. The value at which a datapoint is considered an outlier is determined by the spread of the data for the variable and the researcher's choice on what they consider to be extreme. Seeking to find if you have outliers in your data can often uncover mistakes. For example, if we have a variable that has 5000 participants' ages and 4999 of them range between 18 and 97 but one is 333, logic suggests that this outlier is probably a mistake and we can mark it as missing. For the purpose of this section, we will use common practices to determine outliers for our variables.

Outliers have the ability to strongly influence the results of statistical analysis. For example, if a researcher wanted to know the average price of a home in a neighborhood with 10 homes and all 10 homes were somewhere between $250,000 and $350,000, they could expect the average to be somewhere between $250,000 and $350,000. But what if one house in the neighborhood was a newly built home worth $1.3 million? Or, what if one home had a kitchen fire and the owners abandoned it and let it become dilapidated and run down, so its value is low at $83,000? Could either of those unusual house prices influence the average cost of homes in the neighborhood enough to warrant a closer look at the data?

Although the scenarios above may seem exaggerated, it is indeed possible for an extreme value to skew an entire sample of observations. If we create a spreadsheet for the above three scenarios (Table 2.5), Scenario 2 (having one high outlier) increased the average home price by just over $100,000. Scenario 3, with the low-priced outlier, pulled down the average value of houses in the neighborhood by more than $20,000. However, if the outliers were not included in the calculation the average for the other nine homes was only roughly an $800 difference.

TABLE 2.5 ● AVERAGE HOME VALUE FOR THREE NEIGHBORHOOD SCENARIOS

	Scenario 1	Scenario 2	Scenario 3
Home 1	256000	256000	256000
Home 2	342000	342000	342000
Home 3	267000	267000	267000
Home 4	296000	*1302000*	*83000*
Home 5	308000	308000	308000
Home 6	344000	344000	344000
Home 7	318000	318000	318000
Home 8	290000	290000	290000
Home 9	333000	333000	333000
Home 10	285000	285000	285000
Average (10)	**303900**	**404500**	**282600**
Average (9)		**304777**	**304777**

First, we need to determine if there are any outliers in the data for this variable. One common way to determine if a variable has any outliers is to create a boxplot or histogram figure representation of the variable which can help in determining which datapoints are visually unusual or extreme (these are discussed in more detail in Chapter 5). A frequency table can also be run to determine if there are data values that are extreme. After determining that there are outliers, we decide how to deal with them (e.g., whether we need to remove them or transform the variable measurement in some way).

If we determine that the outliers should be removed, the next step is to create a new variable where we will recode the outliers. For this example, we are going to use the variable emailhr in the GSS data. This variable is made up of responses to the question *about how many hours per week do you spend sending and answering electronic mail or e-mail?* First, we will remove the No answer, Don't know, and Not applicable responses by recoding them to NA.

```
GSS2016$emailhr[GSS2016$emailhr=='-1']=NA
GSS2016$emailhr[GSS2016$emailhr==998]=NA
GSS2016$emailhr[GSS2016$emailhr==999]=NA

hist(GSS2016$emailhr)
```

Output: Histogram for emailhr before removing outliers.

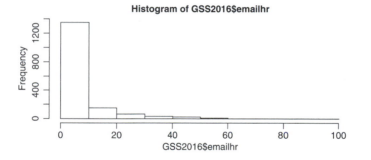

```
boxplot(GSS2016$emailhr, horizontal = FALSE)
boxplot(GSS2016$emailhr, horizontal = TRUE) # Horizontal =
```
FALSE will produce a vertical boxplot, while Horizontal = TRUE will produce a horizontal boxplot.

Output: Vertical and horizontal boxplots for emailhr before removing outliers.

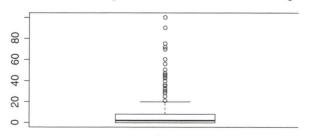

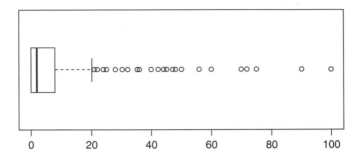

```
boxplot.stats(GSS2016$emailhr)
```

Output: Boxplot Statistics for `emailhr` before removing outliers.

```
$stats
[1]  0  0  2  8  20
# Lower whisker, lower hinge, median, upper hinge, upper whisker.


$n
[1]  1649
# Number of observations (not including NA) in the variable.


$conf
[1]  1.68873  2.31127
# Lower and upper extreme of the notch.


$out
  [1]  40  25  60  45  25  60  44  40  60  50  40  30  50  40  30
 [16]  25  42  90  75  25  22  50  50  40  25  24  32  21  30  30
 [31]  22  30  40  30  50  28  25  56  35  45  40  60  30  60  32
 [46]  30  30  22  21  45  22  70  50  30  40  50  25  25  30  30
 [61]  40  40  35  30  30  47  40  30  40  40  25  40  40  25  35
 [76]  25  35  70  48  28  25  40  30  30  40  40  50  50  25  30
 [91]  30  25  40  30  60  50  25  35  45  35  40  25  30  30  40
[106]  25  30  40  22  30  35  25  35  36  25  50  25  72  30  21
[121]  30  21  40  30  30  50  25  60  100  21  25  48  30  25  42
[136]  50  30  25  30  30  40  30  40
# The suspected outliers—fall beyond the whiskers.
```

```
table(GSS2016$emailhr)
```

Output: Frequency table for `emailhr` before removing outliers

0	1	2	3	4	5	6	7	8	9	10	12	14	15	16	17	18
416	306	183	77	62	92	27	44	42	4	100	27	9	36	3	1	1

20	21	22	24	25	28	30	32	35	36	40	42	44	45	47	48	50
76	5	5	1	24	2	33	2	8	1	25	2	1	4	1	2	13

56	60	70	72	75	90	100
1	7	2	1	1	1	1

```
dataframe$NewVariable<-dataframe$OldVariable[set level or
parameter]
GSS2016$emailhrNoOUT<-GSS2016$emailhr # Creating the new
```
variable emailhrNoOUT from the original variable emailhr.
```
GSS2016$emailhrNoOUT[GSS2016$emailhrNoOUT>26]= NA # Note that
```
we chose to remove values larger than 26, instead of exact values.
```
hist(GSS2016$emailhrNoOUT)  # A histogram of the new variable to
```
compare to the original variable histogram.

Output: Histogram for `emailhrNoOUT` after removing outliers from `emailhr`.

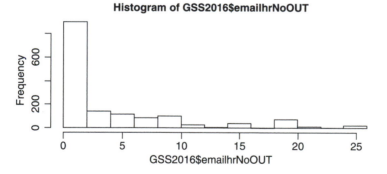

Histogram of GSS2016$emailhrNoOUT

This second histogram gives a much more accurate depiction of the data spread for the majority of the responses.

```
boxplot(GSS2016$emailhrNoOUT, horizontal = F) # Note that the
```
uppercase T or F can be used instead of writing out TRUE or FALSE.
```
boxplot(GSS2016$emailhrNoOUT, horizontal = T)
```

Output: Vertical and horizontal boxplots for `emailhrNoOUT` after removing outliers from `emailhr`.

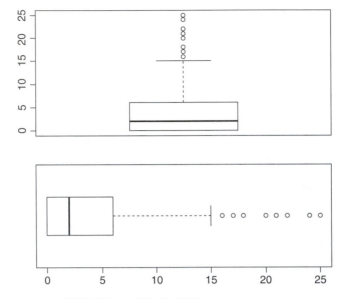

```
boxplot.stats(GSS2016$emailhrNoOUT)
```

Output: Boxplot statistics for `emailhrNoOUT` after removing outliers.

```
$stats
[1]  0  0  2  6  15


$n
[1]  1541
$conf
[1]  1.758506  2.241494


$out
  [1]  25  20  25  20  20  20  20  25  20  20  25  20  22  20  20  25  24  21
       20  22  20
 [22]  20  25  20  20  20  20  20  20  22  21  20  20  22  20  20  20  20  20
       20  20  20
 [43]  25  25  20  20  20  20  17  20  25  20  25  20  20  20  25  20  20  25  20
       20  20
 [64]  20  20  16  20  20  25  25  20  20  25  25  20  20  20  25  20  22  20
       20  25  16
 [85]  20  20  25  20  20  25  20  20  20  21  20  21  20  25  20  20  20  21
       25  20  20
[106]  20  25  20  25  16  18  20  20  20  20  20
```

> **Tip:** Keep in mind that when we remove outliers, our variable measure of central tendency and measure of variability will change. Then, there can be new outliers. So, be attentive when deciding what you choose to remove and why.

```
table(GSS2016$emailhrNoOUT)
```

Output: Frequency table for `emailhrNoOUT` after removing outliers from email.

0	1	2	3	4	5	6	7	8	9	10	12	14	15	16	17	18
416	306	183	77	62	92	27	44	42	4	100	27	9	36	3	1	1

20	21	22	24	25
76	5	5	1	24

If we did not want to make a new variable of the `emailhr` without the outliers, we could also create a new index of the `emailhr` without the outliers (Figure 2.16). This can be useful for immediate analysis of an individual variable, but will not be as helpful when conducting more advanced statistical analyses. The index cannot be saved "within" the dataset because it will have fewer rows. When the number of rows does not match, R cannot join them. All of the same univariate analyses discussed in later chapters, such as frequency tables, histograms, boxplots, and descriptive statistics can be run using this variable that we have created "outside" of the dataset as a separate object.

```
Emailhrwithout26<-(GSS2016$emailhr[GSS2016$emailhr <26])
```

FIGURE 2.16 ● SCREENSHOT OF NEW INDEX **emailhrwithout** AFTER REMOVING OUTLIERS

Looking at the environment window, we can observe a difference in observation numbers (rows). There are 108 responses that have been removed from the data. Those are the 108 outlier responses that were over 26 hours. A second way to deal with outliers is to "top code" the data and impute a "highest value". For example, a researcher might top code `emailhr` at 25 by imputing all values of 26 and over to 25 and referring to the top code simply as "25 or more hours".

Try the process of selecting out portions of the data. Remove or impute any responses above 15 hours. Then, create a histogram and table to double-check.

```
GSS2016$emailhrwithout15<-(GSS2016$emailhr)
GSS2016$emailhrwithout15[GSS2016$emailhr > 15]=NA

hist(GSS2016$emailhrwithout15)
table(GSS2016$emailhrwithout15)

boxplot(GSS2016$emailhrwithout15, horizontal = F)
boxplot(GSS2016$emailhrwithout15, horizontal = T)

boxplot.stats(GSS2016$emailhrwithout15)
Emailhrwithout15<-(GSS2016$emailhr[GSS2016$emailhr <15])
```

A third way to deal with outliers is to "transform" the data so that the outliers will not be lost, but the transformation can help get the data closer to a normal distribution. This is often done when the data are very skewed. Data can be transformed by performing a mathematical computation on the original data. The most common transformations involve polynomials and log transformations. See Chapter 12 to learn how to transform data in RStudio.

CONCLUSION

This chapter offered a review of types of datasets (long vs. wide structures) and levels of variable measurement. We introduced some background of the GSS dataset and codebook, which will be used throughout the rest of the book. We discussed some common procedures in R/RStudio for modifying data, including recoding variables and computing a single value based on responses across multiple variables. We also focused on handling missing data. Other, more advanced techniques for handling of missing data are beyond the scope of this chapter but are discussed more in Chapter 12.

References

Smith, T. W., Davern, M., Freese, J., & Morgan, S. L. (2019). *General Social Surveys, 1972–2018* [Machine-Readable Data File]. Chicago, IL: NORC at the University of Chicago. Retrieved from http://www.gss.norc.org/getthedata/Pages/Home.aspx